D0947211

The   's re-
                                                        m

Linguistic Minorities and Literacy

Trends in Linguistics
Studies and Monographs 26

Editor

Werner Winter

Mouton Publishers
Berlin · New York · Amsterdam

D0947212

Linguistic Minorities and Literacy

Language Policy Issues
in Developing Countries

edited by
Florian Coulmas

Mouton Publishers
Berlin · New York · Amsterdam

CIP-Kurztitelaufnahme der Deutschen Bibliothek

Linguistic minorities and literacy : language policy
issues in developing countries / ed. by Florian Coulmas.
– Berlin ; Amsterdam ; New York : Mouton, 1984.
   (Trends in linguistics : Studies and monographs ; 26)
   ISBN 3-11-009867-9
NE: Coulmas, Florian [Hrsg.] ; Trends in linguistics /
Studies and monographs

Library of Congress Cataloging in Publication Data

Linguistic minorities and literacy.
   Most of the papers are based on presentations given at a
workshop held under the auspices of the United Nations Univer-
sity of Tokyo, Sept. 4-5, 1982.
   Includes index.
   1. Linguistic minorities – Developing countries –
Congresses. 2. Literacy – Developing countries –
Congresses. 3. Language policy – Developing countries –
Congresses. I. Coulmas, Florian. II. United Nations University.
P119.315.L56   1984   409'172'4   84-14746
ISBN 3-11-009867-9

© Copyright 1984 by Walter de Gruyter & Co., Berlin. All rights reserved, including those of translation into foreign languages. No part of this book may
be reproduced in any form – by photoprint, microfilm, or any other means –
nor transmitted nor translated into a machine language without written permission from the publishers. Typesetting: Copo, Bangkok / Werksatz Marschall,
Berlin. Printing: Druckerei Hildebrand, Berlin. – Binding: Dieter Mikolai, Berlin.
Printed in Germany.

To my father
on the occasion of his seventieth birthday

Contents

Preface

Linguistic Minorities, National Languages, and Literacy: Language Policy in Developing Countries was the title of a workshop held under the auspices of the United Nations University in Tokyo, September 4/5, 1982. Most of the papers in this volume grew out of presentations given at the workshop, which was planned to stimulate a broad discussion of problems relating to the precarious situation of linguistic minorities. Of special concern were unwritten minority languages and the question of how their speakers should acquire literacy. By way of preparation, the participants of the meeting were requested to comment on the following questions.

1. Are there any conflicts between the rights of ethnic and linguistic minorities to use and preserve their language and the desire of centralized states to establish a national language as a universal means of communication and administration? If so, can such conflicts be resolved without sacrificing the interests of minority groups? What are the relative values of centralization, on the one hand, and cultural and linguistic variety, on the other hand?
2. Intercultural communication is not only a problem between nations. As ethnically and culturally homogeneous nations are the exception rather than the rule, it is a domestic problem for many states. In how far and how can literacy campaigns for linguistic minorities help to overcome such problems of intercultural communication within centralized national states?
3. If literacy is recognized as a desirable goal for everyone, how can this goal be best achieved for linguistic minorities? What are the factors to be taken into account in deciding in what language literacy should be taught to a linguistic minority? Should linguistic minorities have the right to choose the language in which literacy is taught?
4. What are the social consequences of literacy campaigns carried out in a language other than the mother tongue of those who are/were being subjected to such campaigns?
5. What are the pros and cons of reducing hitherto unwritten languages to writing, and what are the linguistic consequences? What are the main functional differences between spoken and written languages, and in how far can it be expected that hitherto unwritten minority languages will assume the functions of written languages when reduced to writing?
6. According to article 26 of the Declaration of Human Rights, every individual is entitled to adequate education. Should this general appeal be interpreted as implying a human right to literacy, or should literacy rather be considered a contingent right appropriated only to those members of a society who need it to execute their role efficiently?

Obviously, these questions are much too complex to be accounted for conclusively in a two-day meeting. However, they sparked a very fruitful discussion, shedding light on some of the dominant issues. It became evident, in the course of the discussion, that these questions, as well as many others concerning language planning and policy, do not allow for all-encompassing answers. Rather, they must be adapted to the specific socioeconomic, cultural-educational, and linguistic conditions of the countries concerned. Moreover, answers are bound to vary with one's political convictions, as the reader of the chapters in this volume cannot fail to notice.

There are those who are committed to the promotion of national languages or standard languages as a means of nation-building and modernization; and there are those who call for the protection of minorities as a prerequisite of preserving linguistic and cultural multiformity. Ideally, of course, these positions should not be in opposition to each other but combine to form a policy that would satisfy the needs of modern nation-states and yet preserve as much linguistic and cultural variety as possible. Such reconciliation, however, is hard to achieve.

From a general humanistic point of view, linguistic pluralism is preferable to linguistic uniformization and the elimination of languages. From a more practical point of view, the establishment of a standard language is perceived as the more pressing problem by many of the people who are called upon to formulate the language policy of their country.

In view of such differences of perception and attitude, it seems desirable to share the statements presented at the workshop with a wider audience of policy makers, educators, administrators, and linguists, and thus help to provoke more concern for and systematic research on the linguistic and educational problems of linguistic minorities.

The said workshop was sponsored by the United Nations University. As important as the financial support was the personal encouragement and help I received from some of its members. In particular, I owe a debt of gratitude to Kinhide Mushakoji, one of the University's vice-rectors, and Janusz Golebiowski, a senior programme officer. While preparing for the meeting and editing this volume, I received a joint grant from the Japan Society for the Promotion of Science and the Alexander von Humboldt Stiftung, which is also gratefully acknowledged.

F. C.
Tokyo, April 1983

Foreword

KINHIDE MUSHAKOJI, *UNITED NATIONS UNIVERSITY*

The issues of minority languages and literacy campaigns are complex and cannot find adequate solutions without prior scientific inquiry. This book is meant to encourage concerned readers to develop an interest in this problem, which cannot be ignored by anyone who realizes the importance of development. It is also meant to invite linguists and researchers of other social-scientific as well as natural-scientific disciplines to contribute to the research on this multidimensional *problématique*. It is, finally, directed to planners and decision-makers to provide them with a few examples of the complexity of the issues at hand, so that they will avoid making too-facile policy decisions which might affect not only the welfare of the minority peoples but also the very bases of national development.

The problems dealt with in this volume will show why a scientific approach is needed in policy planning. As a matter of fact, the question of how to deal with minority languages in planning literacy campaigns involves delicate choices among alternative policies where the trade-offs are not necessarily self-evident; it is only when enough empirical evidence is at hand that reasonable decisions can be made.

It is true that from the time nation-states began to be formed in Europe, the central governments of states in infancy have felt it necessary to promote single national languages and hence to downgrade the status of all other "minority" languages. It is, however, impossible for the developing countries of today simply to imitate what the early developers in the West did before them. The European models involved entirely different socioeconomic, political, and cultural settings, where national languages were developed first by the sheer force of event, before any conscious policies were adopted by the governments.

Linguistic planning — like all kinds of planning, indeed — is an exercise which cannot ignore the correlations of sociocultural trends and political power relationships, and in today's emerging nation-states it must face a variety of realities which were not present in the West and often are not even comparable from region to region or from country to country. This is why no *a priori* value judgement about either the primacy of the national interest in having one national language or the basic collective right of cultural communities to preserve their own languages, can become the sole basis in linguistic planning. The linguistic policies of the emerging nations should be based on sufficient sociolinguistic information on the minority languages as well as on the national language, and on textual and functional literacy and its implications for social and economic development. This information base would be incomplete without taking into consideration the different sociocultural, political, and economic factors determining the distribution of languages, written and/or spoken. Any policy intervention should, thus, be based on an interdisciplinary analysis of the state of affairs.

This is why it is the responsibility of sociolinguists and their fellow social scientists to pose broadly and boldly the complexity of the problems faced by the linguistic planners conducting a literacy campaign in a multilingual society. In fact, the concerned public should also be conscious of how delicate such policy decisions are, since they are exposed to the two opposed views on paramount national interests and minority rights.

Readers in industrialized countries should not believe that the topics dealt with in this book do not concern their societies. In fact, the growing minorities of immigrants, e.g., the *Gastarbeiter* in Germany and elsewhere, pose anew the problems of linguistic policy — if not literacy campaigns — and minority languages, in a way no less serious than in the recently industrializing countries of the Third World.

The present book will provide, in this context, an introduction into this complex *problématique*. It will show why and how linguists and other social scientists try to study the *problématique*. They sometimes have to ask tough questions of the planners. They also have to indicate alternative policy options.

They have yet another function. More than anything else, they have to speak for the peoples concerned and hence must listen to them first, trying to understand their specific needs and aspirations, as well as the emerging forces which they constitute as a minority within the emerging nations.

As a community of scholars conducting research on the pressing global problems of human survival, development, and welfare, the United Nations University is deeply interested in the problems of national minorities, especially in the context of development planning. This is a major problem within one of its priority themes, "human and social development and coexistence among different cultures and social systems." Since one of the University's objectives is to develop scientific research beyond mere policy science providing technical advice to the planners, it was only natural for it to convoke the contributors to this publication with a view to defining the *problématique* of minority languages and literacy campaigns, especially in order to determine the range of scientific inquiries indispensable for setting up reasonable policies. The University is therefore grateful to Dr. F. Coulmas for his key role in making this dialogue a success and for having launched the foundation of this book.

Linguistic minorities and literacy*

FLORIAN COULMAS, *UNIVERSITÄT DÜSSELDORF*

Language is one of the chief means of social organization and control. In modern times, the *written* language has assumed indispensable functions in this regard, serving as a means of education, law, and information storage and distribution in general. Science and technology depend on writing. The economy, culture, and social structure of the industrialized countries are intimately linked with written communication.

The functions of written language are different from those of speech and, accordingly, societies differ with respect to the extent that communication is carried out by means of spoken or written language. Nearly general literacy is an exclusive achievement of the industrialized countries of the North, while illiteracy is still a major social problem for many developing countries of the South. Many campaigns are being, or have been, carried out in order to eradicate illiteracy. But, in spite of these campaigns, the number of people who are classed as illiterate is still enormous: according to an estimate by UNESCO, in 1980 some 820 million people over the age of fifteen all over the world were illiterate. As literacy expert John Oxenham (1980:2) observes, "the world map of illiteracy coincides very closely with the world map of poverty. The poorer countries of the world tend to have the highest proportions of illiterates." The twenty-five poorest countries of the world show illiteracy rates in excess of 80 per cent. About 70 per cent of all illiterates live in Asia, some 20 per cent in Africa, and about 5 per cent in Latin America.

At the same time, many of the countries with high illiteracy rates are culturally and linguistically heterogeneous, being composed of several different ethnic groups. For many Third World countries these two facts constitute two major social problems:

(i) the problem of eradicating illiteracy;
(ii) the problem of protecting linguistic and cultural minorities.

* Research for this paper was supported by a joint grant of the Japan Foundation for the Promotion of Science and the Alexander von Humboldt Stiftung, which is gratefully acknowledged. Parts of this paper overlap with a report of the United Nations University conference on linguistic minorities and literacy which was prepared for "Development Forum".

How do these two problems interact, and how do their respective solutions affect each other? This is the main question that I want to address in this paper. An answer, or rather partial answers to it, should eventually, both help to improve the efficiency of literacy campaigns and assist minority languages under pressure.

Literacy as a human right

According to article 26 of the Declaration of Human Rights, every individual is entitled to adequate education. While this is not a very clear statement, a reasonable interpretation of its spirit has to take it to imply a human right to literacy. Only literate people are capable of independently acquiring knowledge and conquering ignorance. In modern nation-states only those who are literate have access to and control over the machineries of government, and only they can control the technologies which are changing the wealth, organization, and structure of their societies. Literacy is an indicator of social and economic stratification. In modern states political participation presupposes literacy, despite the growing importance of other media. Literacy is, therefore, to be regarded as a part of the human right to education. Many countries recognize this right, implicitly or explicitly. Its implementation has to be achieved, however, under widely differing conditions.

Historically, the development of mass literacy was correlated with trade, urbanization, the growth of transportation and infrastructure, and in general, with the modes of production. Literacy, in other words, interacts with economic change: it presupposes a certain level of production and its spread, urbanization, the growth of transportation and infrastructure, and, in general, modes of production. Literacy, in other words, interacts with economic change: it presupposes a certain level of production, and its spread, in turn, exercises certain effects on the level of production. To be more specific, production must yield a surplus over subsistence for a society to afford mass literacy. It must be economically possible to free people temporarily from productive work so that they can acquire and practice literary skills. In Europe mass literacy went hand-in-hand with growing prosperity. As has been pointed out tirelessly by scholars such as the late M. McLuhan (1962), J. Goody (1968), H.H. Graff (1981), and many others, the invention of the printing press came at a time when its exploitation was economically feasible and hence had profound effects on the development of the modern Western world. Surplus over subsistence leads to the detachment of labor from domestic food production, higher levels of division of labor and specialization, and urbanized wage labour. Where no economic surplus over subsistence exists, chances for the development of mass literacy and education are slim.

The achievement of nearly general literacy in the West took several hundred years. Much infrastructural development preceded it. Thus, even though literacy may be recognized as a human right, it is an illusion to assume that a nonliterate society will become literate overnight if it only is provided with literacy training. Unless the communicative network and requirements for using language in writing are present, the introduction of the written medium alone cannot be expected to transform a traditional society rapidly into a modern one. Literacy can be a tool of development, but it cannot replace economic measures, and the problem of illiteracy cannot be seen in isolation from other social problems.

Literacy and language

Literacy is not merely a problem of teaching the uneducated masses how to read and write the language that they speak. In some cases literacy campaigns concur with programs for promoting a standard language. In other cases, the problems of illiteracy are further complicated by the fact that the language of the masses has not been a written language until recently. Yet another problem is the multilingualism of many countries. The promotion of a national language is considered by many governments as an important means of increasing national coherence. Also, it can hardly be denied that a multiplicity of languages within one country is an obstacle to trade and the mobility of labour, technology, and information. In certain African and Asian states the multiplicity of languages slows down modernization by impeding dissemination of knowledge and economic integration. It is not surprising, therefore, that national governments have found it advisable to carry out literacy campaigns in (actual or projected) national languages. This issue is especially critical in heterogeneous societies where knowledge and education is unequally distributed among different ethnic groups. There the members of linguistic minority groups are often doubly disadvantaged, as they are not only illiterate but also speakers of a language that has never been provided with a script. Obviously, linguistic diversity of this kind poses serious problems to the administration of literacy campaigns and the establishment of a system of national education. The crucial question here is that of how the respective interests of a centralized state on the one hand and those of ethnic or linguistic minorities on the other hand can be reconciled. Although some countries have made great efforts to solve the various problems relating to this question (China, for instance, has a Central Committee for its national minorities: see Edmondson's paper in this volume), the organisational problems of administering literacy campaigns and language standardization programmes are so vast in some cases that linguistic minorities are not receiving enough attention to secure the preservation of their cultural and linguistic heritage. The main objective of literacy campaigns is to elevate the educational level of the masses, and the road to success, for the individual as well as for the country as a whole, is mostly seen to lead via *literacy in the standard language* or in an otherwise widely-used language.

It is interesting to note in this connection that literacy experts do not usually look at literacy as a linguistic problem. A review, for example, of a recent report of the International Council for Adult Education (ed. H. S. Bhola, 1981) about literacy campaigns reveals a striking ignorance about linguistic problems in general and those of minority languages in particular. These particular problems of linguistic minorities are thus, more often than not, largely neglected by those in charge of literacy campaigns. An indication of this neglect is that illiteracy statistics for individual countries are only rarely broken down according to the mother tongues of the population concerned.

Linguistic minorities, minority languages

Less than 4 % of all peoples live within boundaries coinciding with the extension of their ethnic groups. Consequently, the populations of most countries include one or several minorities. At the present time, the world is divided into some 160 nation-states, a number that is only a small fraction of that of the world's living languages, numbering in the thousands. To establish an exact number is out of the question, for many languages are hardly known, and in many cases it is difficult to draw a clear-cut distinction between language and dialect. Moreover, it has proved a formidable task to establish uniform criteria for distinguishing languages and dialects from each other. But, although exact numbers are thus unavailable, estimates range between five and eight thousand, and no serious index lists fewer than four thousand languages spoken throughout the world (see, e.g., Grimes 1978; Voegelin and Voegelin 1977). The great majority of these languages are spoken by very small populations, minority groups living in states dominated by speakers of more widely-spoken languages, such as English, Spanish, Russian, Hindi, or Chinese. The linguistic composition of the world is characterized by a great disparity between number of languages and number of speakers of these languages (cf. Table 1). Nevertheless, there is hardly a state that does not have one or several minorities. In fact, monolingual states are extremely rare (for instance Iceland or Tonga). Worldwide, states where more than one language is spoken are the vast majority (cf. Table 2). Some of these minority languages are spoken by only a few hundred speakers while others have millions of speakers. What will be the future of these minorities and

TABLE 1: Languages and World Population

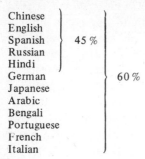

Chinese
English
Spanish   } 45 %
Russian
Hindi
German   } 60 %
Japanese
Arabic
Bengali
Portuguese
French
Italian

25 languages account for 75 % of the world's population.
± 100 languages account for 95 % of the world's population.

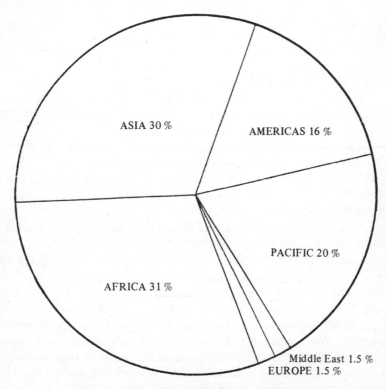

ASIA 30 %

AMERICAS 16 %

PACIFIC 20 %

AFRICA 31 %

Middle East 1.5 %
EUROPE 1.5 %

DISTRIBUTION OF LANGUAGES IN THE WORLD
BY CONTINENT (slightly adapted from Grimes 1978)

their languages? Clearly, this question ought to be of major concern to administrators and politicians involved in the educational and linguistic policy of their country. As most of the languages in question are spoken in developing countries, it is also an important issue of development policy (see chart above).

When discussing the future of groups that perceive themselves as "minorities" within the fabric of a nation, several types of minorities have to be distinguished. One of the most obvious and least controversial criterion for defining a minority group is its mother tongue. However, even this criterion covers a range of different minority groups. There is a significant difference, first of all, between 'linguistic minorities' and 'the speakers of a minority language'. The concept of 'linguistic minority' refers to the relative part that the speakers of a language constitute within the total population of a country. Thus the Francophone Canadians are a linguistic minority in Canada, and the

TABLE 2: Languages per Country

no. of languages	no. of countries	percentage of countries of the world
1	6	4 %
2	22	14 %
3 – 5	27	18 %
6 – 50	24	16 %
11 – 50	46	30 %
over 50	28	18 %

Tamil-speaking Indians are a linguistic minority in Singapore and several other countries in Asia and Africa. French and Tamil, however, are the mother tongues of 75 million and 45 million speakers, respectively. By 'minority language', in contrast, we mean minor languages that do not serve as standard or national languages in any country.

More specifically, we are concerned with languages that, in the nation state in which they are spoken, are not an appropriate means of vertical mobility and full participation in national life. Given such a tentative definition, it is clear that some "minority languages" are really major languages in terms of numbers of speakers (cf. Bamgboṣe's paper in this volume). This state of affairs is particularly common in recently decolonized countries that continue to use the language of their former colonial masters as an official or even national language. In countries such as, Nigeria, Cameroon, or New Guinea, where languages range in the hundreds, no autochthonous language may have majority status and the former colonial language may indeed be the language most widely-understood in the country. In such cases, of course, not all of the autochthonous languages should indiscriminately be regarded as minority languages. The survival chances of languages with a speech community of many millions are obviously much better than those of languages with very small populations.

Another important distinction is that between written and unwritten languages. As the history of Europe exemplifies, modern nationhood is anchored in one dominant language that is provided with a written standard. Establishing such a written standard or national language often went along with considerable suppression of and discrimination against linguistic minorities (cf., e.g., Calvet 1974). The idea of the nation-state and with it the European nationalism that has flourished since the Renaissance has never favoured linguistic and cultural diversity, but rather stressed unity and uniformity. Minorities were often seen as a threat to national integrity (Deutsch 1953).

Nowadays, many recently independent countries appear to follow the European example. Nationalism is considered an important instrument of nation-building on the road to modernization of Third World countries, and it can rarely be reconciled with all of the complex problems of multilingual and multicultural societies. The question, however, is whether the suppression or even elimination of minority languages is a necessary by-product of national consolidation and modernization.

Recently, the problems of cultural and linguistic minorities have received much attention, especially in Western Europe and in the United States, where minority peoples are becoming increasingly conscious of the threats that centralized governments and educational systems pose to their cultural and linguistic identity. Will it be possible for national states in the Third World whose centralized authority has yet to be established, to learn from the problems encountered by polylinguistic societies in northern hemisphere countries?

To mention but one example, take the Occitan minority in France. The Occitan community is very conscious of its language and values it highly. However, since the Renaissance and the central government's drive toward general literacy in France, it has been under constant pressure by French, which has been and is the medium of literacy. Before French became established as the only national language in France, Occitan was a highly cultivated language whose poetic tradition in the Middle Ages was older and more refined than that of French. French, however, was the dialect of power, and, through its establishment as the national language, all other languages of France were reduced to "jargons". Nevertheless, in modern times attempts were made at using Occitan for literary purposes too, but for lack of coordination two very different written varieties of the language have evolved. This is of course an unfortunate result of the efforts to protect and preserve a minority language by providing it with a written standard. Unless, however, such a task is entrusted to some recognized authority that might put its weight behind newly codified norms, similar results are likely to occur.

The vast majority of minority languages are unwritten languages, whose speakers will have to decide eventually whether or not they should become written languages. During the past 50 years, linguists have provided many languages with suitable scripts. This fact, however, does not in itself make a written language out of a hitherto unwritten language. By "written language" we mean a language that has an autochthonous literary tradition. In pursuit of their own ideological purposes missionaries have played an important role in "reducing" many hitherto unwritten languages to writing. But this does not imply in many cases that the speakers of the respective languages have become literate. It has been pointed out repeatedly that people with little contact with the affairs of literate societies experience small need or desire for literacy. Providing a language with a suitable script is only one of the many conditions of turning a traditional society into a literate one.

From a sociological point of view, languages that are not used in written communication by their speakers are to be considered unwritten languages, regardless of whether or not they have been "reduced to writing" by a linguist. Linguistic minorities of such languages are in a particularly precarious situation, because they are not equipped with linguistic means appropriate for meeting the challenges of the transition from traditional to modern societies. Their languages lack the historical, political, and social prestige and protection of literacy; they lack a standard; and they lack the vocabulary of the technological age. Yet they are a major integrating and unifying factor, and in many cases a symbol of the identity of their speakers, enjoying a more frequent and intensive use among them than the superimposed national language of the area in question. The pressure on such minority languages stems from the limited geographical range of their application and the necessity for their speakers to learn the majority or standard language in order to be able to receive a higher education and thus get ahead in society. In some cases, migration to the urban centres is an additional factor contributing to the decline of minority languages.

Such languages are endangered in a very real and concrete sense. Not a few of them are on the brink of becoming extinct; many others have already ceased to exist. This trend may very well be aggravated under the impression of the need for their speakers to become literate in a language other than their mother tongue.

The principal question that arises here is whether this trend — could it be substantiated — should be accepted as a historical fact, or whether, alternatively, measures should be sought to intervene and arrest this decline.

It is hardly possible to give a general answer to this question, because it depends on political and economic considerations as well as on the maybe romantic idea of preserving the multiformity of human culture.

For most governments, literacy campaigns are a considerable financial burden, and they tend to favour the development of mass literacy programmes to the extent that they generate economic benefits. In keeping with this principle, UNESCO, the largest promoter of literacy in developing nations, has focussed its efforts on promoting "functional literacy". This approach hinges on the combination of literacy training with community development projects. It was pointed out above that literacy should not and cannot be seen in isolation from other social and developmental problems. Thus the "functional literacy" approach clearly points in the right direction. It was justly criticized, however, for paying too little attention to linguistic and pedagogical considerations (cf., e.g., Gudschinsky 1976, Calvet 1974). Literacy, after all, is not only an economic problem but also has linguistic, cultural, and sociopsychological aspects whose neglect eventually reduces the chances of carrying out literacy campaigns successfully (cf. Coulmas 1983).

It must also be noted that the assessment of the economic payoff of literacy campaigns is extremely difficult, as it can hardly be measured in isolation from other educational efforts and achievements. One thing is clear, however: cost and benefit considerations put linguistic minorities of unwritten languages at a disadvantage from the very beginning. As a consequence, becoming literate, for many linguistic minorities, implies becoming literate in a language other than their native language, because no literacy training is available in these minority languages. Again, this puts them at a disadvantage relative to the respective majority whose members have to master the script only, and not another language on top of it. The question arises, therefore, as to how this situation, which is typical for many countries, affects the social and economic chances of linguistic minorities, on the one hand, and the status and development of minority languages, on the other hand. Are they affected by literacy campaigns in majority languages, and if so, in what way?

History provides many examples of societies that experienced radical changes due to sudden inroads of writing into their cultural life (cf. Wollock 1980). As a matter of fact, such changes have not always been positive. Since the reduction of "primitive" languages to writing has been closely connected with religious efforts at proselytizing and saving the "savages' " souls, it has more often than not been a prelude to the disruption if not destruction of traditional societies. It is also conceivable that introduction of literacy into a traditional society *without* any ideological byplay on the part of missionaries has an alienating effect, such that the traditional value system which is orally expressed and transmitted from one generation to the next loses its integrating power. While this is not necessarily to be condemned or deplored, it is certainly reasonable to try to anticipate the consequences and reflect on the values that will most likely replace the traditional ones. Literacy is undoubtedly one of the major forces of transforming traditional societies, but so far we know very little about the consequences of literacy for unwritten languages and their speakers.

Literacy and modernization

The transition from traditional to modern societies is marked, and to some extent caused, by literacy and its spreading since the invention of the printing press. Scholars such as Marshall McLuhan and Jack Goody have investigated and discussed in great detail the historical and social implications of a visual instead of an oral organisation of knowledge. The development of the phonetic alphabet and the invention of printing with moveable types were major steps toward the emergence of modern societies in the Western world, where literacy, as Jack Goody (1968) says, has become the "technology of the intellect." One of the consequences of literacy, which has, however, not received very much attention, is the standardization of languages. Modern English, French, German, Italian, etc., are the results of deliberate efforts at standardization since the Renaissance. As opposed to this, the unwritten languages spoken in the many recently decolonized countries of Africa and Asia are mostly unstandardized and exhibit a much greater diversity of usage. The relationship between writing and standardization is not yet very well understood, but while certain unwritten languages have been known to achieve a standard form recognized by their speakers, it is undoubtedly true that writing is an important aid to standardization. Of course, language standardization is a dynamic process, and a standardized language is the result of a rather long historical development. Selecting a dialect and providing it with an alphabet does not turn that dialect into a standard language. The spread and acceptance of that variety in substantial parts of the speech community are necessary – usually a process that takes many decades rather than years.

Embarking on a programme to establish a new standard language is a decision of great consequence which in effect may slow down the development of a country. This is one reason why many countries continue to use former colonial languages as official or national languages instead of the vernacular, which is not yet deemed fit for communication purposes of modern life. On the other hand, many countries, such as, e.g., Indonesia, Tanzania, Somalia, and the Philippines, have decided to forge a vernacular language into a standardized language and substitute it for English, French, German, Italian, Dutch, or whatever the colonial language had been. In these countries the national language is given precedence over all other languages spoken within their boundaries, in the interests of creating a national identity. This is politically understandable if seen from the point of view of central authority; but it can hardly be denied that the striving for national identity in multi-ethnic and multilingual societies often clashes with the forces and dynamics which govern ethno-cultural identity. Literacy is a precondition to modernization, as it makes systematic education possible; but it cannot be achieved against the resistance of the people.

Different peoples have different attitudes towards their native languages. Some societies entertain very strong feeling about and sentimental attachments to their language as a symbol of identity. These factors have to be taken into account in order to avert unnecessary resistance against literacy campaigns by those who could potentially benefit from them, as their participation in modern life will be facilitated.

It is also important to realize that by no means all linguistic minorities want literacy training in their mother tongues. Literacy in minority languages is frequently resented by their speakers, because it forces them into segregation and they feel that their language is only of limited modern utility. On the other hand, there are also communities who desire that their languages become written languages and be used for literacy training and primary education. They should be given the necessary financial and administrative assistance. Thus the officials who are responsible for designing and implementing the linguistic and educational policy in developing countries are faced with a very intricate dilemma, because the preferences for literacy in national or minority languages are divided for both the central authority and the minority groups themselves. The policy of enforcing a national language is often opposed by minorities for political or ideological reasons. But a policy that respects and reinforces the identity of minorities by tolerating their languages may inadvertently diminish the chances of the minority language speakers to participate in the economic, cultural, and political life of the country at large.

Imposing a standard (national, regional) language on a linguistic minority means to force its members to learn and use a language they do not consider their own, to carry out all kinds of social functions in that language, and to recognize it in this regard as the most important medium of linguistic interaction. Such a policy may lead to discouraging or even suppressing the use of the minority language.

A more liberal policy, on the other hand, where the central government does not enforce a standard language as a subject and medium of education, but instead adopts a laissez-faire attitude allowing every language group to use its language in whatever social domain it wants, may in effect aggravate the disadvantages of such minority groups. Not being forced to learn the majority language, they are actually being deprived of a prerequisite of participating in many social domains and economic undertakings.

Similarly difficult is the question of whether or not literacy should be promoted in minority languages. Reserving the written medium to only one or some of the languages of a country is tantamount to furnishing these languages with more prestige and importance than those vernacular languages that are not written. On the other hand, if a language has been provided with a script only recently, it is questionable whether its speakers would benefit much from becoming literate in that language, because there is little reading material with which they can then practice their newly acquired ability. It is understandable, therefore, that in most countries literacy is promoted in or alongside the respective national language. In this sense, a national language is always privileged over minority languages, and the promotion of literacy is thus a potential threat to the cultural heritage of minority peoples with unwritten languages. The question, however, is whether a language that is superior in terms of social strength and the communication network it makes accessible *has* to be in conflict with the maintenance and development of minority languages.

Functional allocations for different languages in multilingual communities are not uncommon and should be possible wherever minorities are eager to preserve their identity. As yet, the conditions for such a policy do not exist everywhere, and in some countries discrimination against minorities and their languages are common practice. There is a valid law, for instance, in Australia's state Victoria that forbids any language other than English as a medium of instruction in school (Neustupný, pers. comm.). A similar law that would make English the only recognized national language of the US is supported by many members of Congress. Thus the plight of linguistic minorities is not only to be found in Third World countries. But it is particularly dramatic there, at present, because many of these countries are still in the process of consolidating their national identity and establishing a national educational system. Moreover, they often lack the financial resources for proper literacy education of even the majority population. Under such circumstances, the specific problems of linguistic minorities are, literally, minor problems.

An important aspect of doing justice to linguistic minorities, however, is that it is less a question of money, and more a question of tolerance and a change of consciousness. If cultural diversity and a multiplicity of languages are taken as a positive value, and if it is recognized that the question of whether or not a given minority culture or language will disappear has its answer in a historical process resulting from specific policy decisions rather than "natural" tendencies of convergence, it becomes easier to promote or maintain bi- and multilingualism in culturally diverse societies.

Eventually, the linguistic minorities concerned should have their say about these questions and be given the right to decide or at least partake in the language policy that will determine the fate of their language. For the time being, it seems doubtful that the particular problems of minority languages have been given enough attention by those responsible for literacy campaigns and national language policy. Yet many developing countries have recently become more aware of the value of local languages and begun to rethink the policy of establishing a national language at the cost of minority languages. The implementation of a policy designed to achieve both modernization and preservation of linguistic and cultural multiformity is an extremely difficult task, needing careful preparation. Much further research is necessary in many countries in order to determine the present role of minority languages in the society at large and the prospects of their speakers to participate in modern life. Criteria will have to be defined for deciding in what language literacy should be taught for every individual case. *That* literacy should be taught is hardly debatable, because, even though the peak of literacy seems to have been passed in some industrialized countries, where literacy has begun to decline under the impact of other media, there can be no doubt that it will play, for decades to come, a crucial role in education and hence in the transformation of traditional societies.

Countries with more than 10 languages (map)

Algeria, Angola, Benin, Botswana, Cameroon, Central African Republic, Chad, Congo, Ethiopia, Gabon, Gambia, Ghana, Guinea, Guinea-Bissau, Ivory Coast, Kenya, Liberia, Malawi, Mali, Mozambique, Namibia, Niger, Nigeria, Senegal, Sierra-Leone, South Africa, Sudan, Tanzania, Togo, Uganda, Upper Volta, Zaire, Zambia, Zimbabwe

Afghanistan, Bangladesh, Burma, China, India, Indonesia, Iran, Iraq, Kampuchea, Laos, Malaysia, Nepal, Pakistan, Philippines, Taiwan, Thailand, Turkey, Vietnam

USA, Canada, Argentina, Bolivia, Brazil, Chile, Colombia, Ecuador, Guatemala, Guyana, Mexico, Paraguay, Peru, Surinam, Venezuela

USSR

Australia

Papua New Guinea, Solomon Islands, Vanuatu, New Caledonia, Kiribati, Nauru, Micronesia (U.S. Trust Territory)

Legend

more than 10
languages per
country

illiteracy
over 40 % of
population

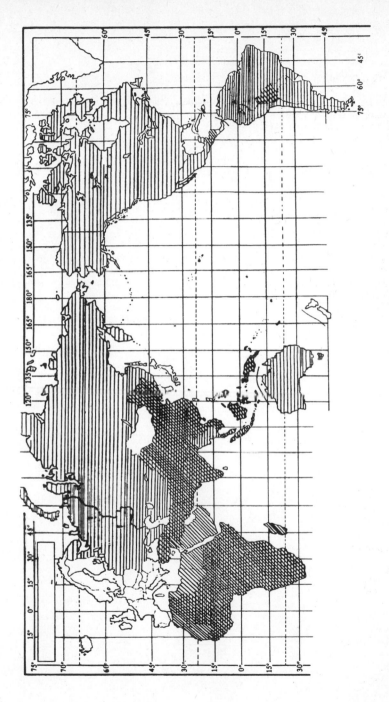

20   *Florian Coulmas*

References

Bhola, H. S., ed. 1981. *Campaigning for Literacy. Report of a study submitted to UNESCO.* International Council for Adult Education.

Calvet, L.-J. 1974. *Linguistique et colonialisme, petit traite de glottophagie.* Paris: Edition Payot.

Coulmas, F., ed. 1983. Linguistic Problems of Literacy. Special issue, *Journal of Pragmatics* 7/5.

Deutsch, K. W. 1953. *Nationalism and Social Communication.* New York.

Goody, J., ed. 1968. *Literacy in Traditional Societies.* London: Cambridge University Press.

Graff, H. H., ed. 1981. *Literacy and Social Development in the West: A Reader.* London: Cambridge University Press.

Grimes, E. F., ed. 1978. *Ethnologue.* Huntington Beach, CA: Wycliffe Bible Translators, Inc.

Gudschinsky, S. C. 1976. *Literacy: The Growing Influence of Linguistics.* The Hague: Mouton.

McLuhan, M. 1962. *The Gutenberg Galaxy: The Making of Typographic Man.* London: Routledge.

Oxenham, J. 1980. *Literacy, Writing, Reading and Social Organization.* London: Routledge & Kegan Paul.

Voegelin, C. F. and Voegelin, F. M. 1977. *Classification and Index of the World's Languages.* New York: Elsevier.

Wollock, J. 1980. William Thornton and the Practical Applications of New Writing Systems. In: R. W. Rieber, ed., *Psychology of Language and Thought.* New York: Plenum Press, pp. 121–151.

Minority languages and literacy

AYỌ BAMGBOṢE, *UNIVERSITY OF IBADAN*

The division of languages into "majority" and "minority" languages is characterized by three features. Firstly, it is generally arbitrary. In most cases, it is
based on numbers of speakers, but sometimes it is based on other considerations such as literary, political, or educational status. Nigeria, for example,
recognizes three major languages out of a total of almost 400 languages.
These three languages – Hausa, Yoruba and Igbo – are also the languages
with the largest number of speakers. Although they share with a fourth
language, Efik, a comparable literary tradition, this language is excluded from
majority status on account of the number of speakers.[1] On the other hand,
Ghana recognizes four majority languages: Twi, Fante (both constituting a
dialect cluster of Akan), Ewe, and Ga on the basis of a written tradition as
well as their status as examination subjects at the end of a secondary school
course.[2] This accounts for the exclusion of two other languages, Guan and
Adangbe, which have a larger number of speakers than Ga.[3]

Secondly, the distinction between majority and minority languages is
relative. For instance, a language which is considered a minority language
at the national level may assume the status of a major language at the state
level. For example, although, as we have seen above, Efik does not qualify
as a major Nigerian language, it is the major language of the Cross River State
of Nigeria. Similarly, a minority language in one country may be larger than
a majority language in another country. For example, practically all of
Ghana's four major languages are smaller than several of Nigeria's minority
languages.[4]

Thirdly, although the term "minority language" tends to convey the
impression of smallness in terms of numbers of speakers, the combined
strength of linguistic minorities in a country may add up to a large number
of speakers. Thus, Nigeria's minority languages account for roughly 36.8 %
of the population, while Ghana's account for 44 %.[5]

The dichotomy between major and minority is only meaningful in the context of the alloted function of a language in a country's language policy. For example, a major language may be a national language, a language used in secondary and higher education, or in communication and administration at the national level. Similarly, a minority language may be one used in primary education and adult literacy. Reporting on literacy in the U.S.S.R., Desheriev gives a tripartite classification of that country's languages into major, medium-sized, and minority. The first type is used at all levels of education, the second type up to secondary school level, and the third type in elementary education and adult literacy only.[6] In this sort of scheme, which has much to recommend it, no language is without its own alloted function. The difference between the so-called minority languages and the major ones is in the narrower scope of roles and alloted functions. And it is possible for the scope of use to be broadened as part of a deliberate policy of creating a literate environment.

Literacy itself must be seen in the context of a country's language policy. In the case of Nigeria, the 1979 Constitution recognizes the three major languages in addition to English at the national level. These languages may be used for proceedings in the National Assembly. At the state level, the main language or languages of the state together with English, will perform a similar role in the state legislative assemblies. The National Policy on Education prescribes the mother tongue or the language of the immediate community as the medium of instruction initially in the primary school. It also envisages that each child should learn one of the three major languages other than his own mother tongue. Although the Policy is silent on the languages to be used in literacy classes, it stipulates that "in character and content all mass literacy programmes will be adapted in each case to local cultural and sociological conditions".[7] This could be interpreted to mean that local languages will be used in literacy, as is generally the practice in the country.

Another important factor that may influence the choice of language for literacy is the goal envisaged for the literacy programme. In this connection, it is usual for literacy specialists to make a distinction between traditional literacy and functional literacy. According to the UNESCO Survey, *Literacy 1969–1971,* traditional literacy can be offered in isolation; it is aimed at all illiterates; its goal is essentially humanistic and the adult is declared literate once he has passed the relevant literacy tests. On the other hand, functional literacy is part of a broader development effort, it is consciously selective (since it is offered to those who can benefit and contribute most to development as a result of being literate), it is more than just work-orientated knowledge, and it is merely the first step in a continuing process of learning.[8]

Traditional literacy has usually been the domain for the utilization of mother tongues, including most of the minority languages. Learning to read, write, and count is best achieved using a language that an illiterate person already speaks well. Hence the role of the linguist in such an endeavour is a primary one, particularly where the language to be used is yet to be reduced to writing. With the shift in emphasis to functional literacy, the choice of language may be dependent on other factors such as utility in the work situation or in a wider community. Thus, in a rural community, the local language may be the choice for improving farming skills, while in an urban situation, a second language may be the choice, for example, in improving the skills of the factory worker.[9]

The emphasis on functional literacy has led to equating concerns in literacy with agricultural extension, occupational training, health, and rural development schemes, and the limitation of literacy materials to immediate needs in a job or in the community. Apart from literacy specialists, the persons believed to be most relevant in functional literacy are the specialists in all these subject areas. In Nigeria, for example, a mass literacy campaign designed to eradicate illiteracy in a period of ten years was scheduled to take off in September 1982; yet in all the planning so far, there has been no input at all by specialists in linguistics. It is important to stress that literacy, by whatever name it is called, is primarily still tied to language skills. As Stanford rightly observes, "reading and writing are still the essential core of literacy and ... it is misleading to define or describe literacy in any way which could be understood as implying that these are in any sense optional or subsidiary".[10]

It is now generally accepted that literacy must be an aspect of the general development process. But such development cannot be narrowly defined in socioeconomic terms. Its goal must be man himself and the full realization of the human potential. One important aspect of national development is mass participation. In this respect, literacy programmes face a dilemma in countries where the official language is a foreign language (as is the case in all West African countries). On the one hand, it is hardly feasible for the foreign official language to be the language of literacy, for there is already the serious problem of inadequacy of teachers, even in the formal school system. On the other hand, literacy in a local or minority language may restrict participation to the local community which is a negation of the principle of mass participation. One possible solution, though admittedly a partial one, is to extend the scope of use of the nonofficial languages, particularly to those domains that touch on the lives of the average citizen. For example, information bulletins, licences, tax receipts, court summonses, and forms required to be completed for various purposes could be made available in as many languages as possible in which the citizens are literate. The media should also contain adequate material directed to such citizens.

In the Declaration of Persepolis, literacy is considered to be "a contribution to the development of man, and to his full development". It is "not an end in itself. It is a fundamental human right".[11] In other words, no one should be denied the right to literacy. In a way, this is at variance with the idea of functional literacy as selective and limited to those who can benefit most from being literate. It should not be difficult at all to accept the declaration that literacy is a fundamental human right. Any contrary view will be to condemn some citizens as being unworthy of becoming literate. So far, it has not been proved that anyone who has become literate has been the worse for it. Rather, there is overwhelming evidence to the contrary of advantages conferred by literacy. The implication of this is that every country should strive to eradicate illiteracy. The only issue at stake is whether this can be achieved in all the languages of the country. Knowing what is involved in the use of a language for literacy work (initial linguistic research, devising of orthography, curriculum design, preparation of materials, traning of teachers, provision of teaching aids, etc.), it should be perfectly acceptable if a language of the immediate community already spoken by a group of people were to be used for literacy instead of the mother tongue.

It is well to remember that many governments in developing countries face the dilemma of having to choose between greater investment in the formal school system or in adult education. The oft-quoted remark by President Nyerere of Tanzania in 1967 that "We must first teach the adults. It will be five, ten or even twenty years before our children have any effect on our economic development"[12] is a minority view, for most African countries concentrate more on the formal school system and only allow adult education to be run on a shoestring. In this sort of situation, it is idle to expect that literacy work can be conducted in all languages. The other extreme of advocating literacy in only one language as typified by the following statement: "a few countries in Africa are making some headway in their efforts by using only *one* national language .... What is needed in every West African country is then some unity of language in the fight against illiteracy"[13] is also not feasible.

The main argument against the use of minority languages in literacy is the cost factor. The various activities required in using a language for literacy work are expensive, and the cost of using several such languages is likely to be prohibitive. At least, so the argument goes. But several factors are ignored in this argument. Local interest may account for a substantial input. For example, local language committees may contribute teachers, writers, and even financial subsidy; there are other interested agencies such as missionary groups which are engaged in literacy work, particularly in minority languages (for example, the Summer Institute of Linguistics); and the cost of producing materials may not be as excessive as is often suggested.

Nigeria, with an estimated population of 80 million, has an estimated illiterate adult population of 30 million. It has been suggested that, with adequate facilities and teachers, the country could achieve a literacy rate of 6 million per annum.[14] Current enrolment figures per annum in government-sponsored literacy cleasses are under 1 million. Given the large number of languages in the country and the fact that there are millions of illiterate adults who do not speak any of the country's major languages, it follows that several minority languages will have to be employed in any effective mass literacy campaign.

The present practice in literacy work in Nigeria is to employ several languages in the heterogeneous states. For example, in Benue State three languages – Tiv, Igala, and Idoma – are used in literacy classes. In addition, several smaller languages are used in private, missionary-sponsored literacy classes all over the country. There is already, therefore, a wealth of experience in the techniques and problems of using such languages for literacy. A particularly significant experience is the one gained from the Rivers Readers Project which was designed to develop initial literacy materials for school populations ranging from just over 1,000 to about 40,000. This project, which was launched in 1977, has succeeded in providing materials for twenty languages/dialects.[15] Two of the methods used in this project may well be copied for adult literacy work. First, language committees working with specialists were used to agree on an orthography, and to go over drafts of readers and primers. Second, a common format (including illustrations) was used for the readers, the only difference being in the language material itself. In order to reduce costs, texts handwritten by an artist and reproduced by offset lithography were preferred to glossy print. Teachers' Notes were also in mimeographed form. Although the content of adult literacy materials will be different from that of this project, the use of similar methods is likely to bring down costs considerably and make possible the use of many smaller languages for literacy work.

The mass literacy campaign beginning in 1982, to which reference has already been made above, is designed as a functional literacy programme firstly to achieve a "total eradication of illiteracy" and secondly "to encourage individuals to see literacy as a means of self-improvement" and "improved performance in their jobs".[16] This immediately raises the question of language. As mentioned earlier, the huge size of the illiterate population and the multilingual situation demand the use of several languages in literacy; the job-orientated functional component may also require that a major language or English is also employed. Unfortunately, not much attention has been given to this question beyond the decision of the Mass Literacy Task Force that the language of instruction during the first phase of the campaign should be the local language (each local task force determining which language or languages) and that the second phase would involve the official language or a second language. The task force also agreed that no particular language (including English) is to be imposed on any state. Rather, "core materials" should be developed in all the main Nigerian languages. Needless to say, these general guidelines will need to be translated into concrete measures, if meaningful results are to be expected from the mass literacy programme.[17]

When everything possible has been done, it is very likely that speakers of certain minority languages will have to be subjected to literacy in another language. If this language is not one that they already speak, a transitional period in which they acquire basic literacy skills in a language they already speak is absolutely essential, for no one should be forced to learn to read and write while at the same time learning a new language code.

Notes

1. Based on the 1963 census the numbers of Hausa, Yoruba, and Igbo native speakers were 11.6 million, 11.3 million and 9.2 million, respectively. Since most of the persons recorded as Fulani in the census are also native speakers of Hausa (never having learnt to speak Fula), the figure for Hausa could be taken to be about 14.6 million. Efik is the written form of Efik-Ibibio with 2.17 million speakers.
2. See Apronti and Denteh 1969.
3. According to the figures from the 1960 census, numbers of native speakers for the languages were as follows: Twi-Fante 2.657 million, Ewe 0.876 million, Guan 0.254 million, Adangbe 0.237 million, and Ga 0.236 million. (Figures taken from Smock 1974.)
4. Assuming Asante to be about 1.662 million in relation to Fante 0.995 million, at least Nigeria's Kanuri 2.26 million, Efik 2.17 million, are larger than Ghana's largest major language; and there are still others like Tiv 1.39 million, Ijo 1.08 million, Edo 0.95 million, not to talk of several other languages, which are much larger than Ghana's smallest major language, Ga.
5. These percentages represent only those who speak the major languages concerned as a first language. If the number of those who speak them as a second language is added, the percentages would probably be larger by half.
6. See Desheriev 1973.
7. Federal Republic of Nigeria *National Policy on Education* 1981: 32.
8. Extracts from *Literacy 1969–1971* are quoted in Stanford 1981: 175.
9. For example, in Nigeria functional literacy has been conducted in Yoruba for improving the skills of tobacco and maize farmers. Hagan has also reported the use of English in literacy classes in Sierra Leone for specific target groups such as taxi drivers, industrial workers, and domestic servants. See Hagan 1979: 200.
10. Stanford op. cit. 179.

11. The Declaration of Persepolis is the set of conclusions adopted by the International Symposium for Literacy held at Persepolis on September 3–8, 1975. The text of the Declaration is reproduced in full in Hummel 1977, pp. 68, 70, 72, 74.
12. Hummel op. cit. 73.
13. Hagan op. cit. 204.
14. See N. E. R. C. 1980: 120.
15. For a full report on the planning and execution of this project see Williamson 1975 and Williamson 1976.
16. Federal Republic of Nigeria op. cit. 32.
17. I am grateful to Dr. Ọmọlẹwa for information on the decisions of the Mass Literacy Task Force on language. There is also some discussion of the language question in Akinde and Ọmọlẹwa 1982: 71–93.

References

Akinde, C. O. and M. Ọmọlẹwa 1982. Background issues relating to the proposed Mass Literacy Campaign in Nigeria. *International Review of Education XXVIII*, 71–93.

Apronti, E. O. and A. C. Denteh 1969. Minority Languages. In: Birnie, J. H. and G. Ansre, eds. 1969. *Proceedings of the conference on the study of Ghanaian languages.* Accra: Institute of African Studies, University of Ghana.

Bamgboṣe, A. ed. 1976. *Mother Tongue Education: The West African Experience.* London: Hodder & Stoughton.

Desheriev, Y. S. 1973. Language policy and principles of definition of relative language utility. In: *Anthropology and Language Science in Educational Development.* UNESCO Educational Studies and Documents No. 11, Paris: Unesco.

Federal Republic of Negeria *National Policy on Education 1981. (Revised)*, Lagos: Federal Government Press (first published 1977).

Hagan, K. O. 1979. Literacy efforts in West Africa. In: L. Bown and S. H. O. Tomori, eds. *A Handbook of Adult Education for West Africa.* London: Hutchinson.

Hummel, C. 1977. *Education today for the world of tomorrow.* Paris: Unesco.

N. E. R. C. (Nigeria Educational Research Council) 1980. *Perspectives on quantities and qualities in Nigerian education.* Lagos: N. E. R. C.

Smock, D. R. 1974. Language Policy in Ghana. In: D. R. Smock and K. Bentsi-Enchill, eds. 1974. *The search of national integration in Africa.* New York: The Free Press.

Stanford, R. 1981. Language and adult education with special emphasis on adult literacy. In: L. Bown and J. T. Okedara, eds. 1981. *An introduction to the study of adult education.* Ibadan: Ibadan University Press.

Williamson, K. 1975. *Small languages in primary education: the Rivers Readers Project.* African Languages 5.2: 95–105.

Williamson, K. 1976. The Rivers Readers Project in Nigeria. In: Bamboṣe, ed. 1976.

Consequences of initiating literacy in the second language

R. N. SRIVASTAVA, *UNIVERSITY OF DELHI*

Literacy assumed here can be defined as a communication skill which involves a written mode of verbal transmission employed by "literate" societies for effective functioning in their ever-proliferating socioecological setting. Viewed from the aspect of linguistic resources, literacy may be regarded as an extension of the functional potential of language with regard to the channel of communication which involves reading and writing skills. The ethnography of literacy views this extension in the mode of verbal transmission as a primary instrument of change in the "world-view" (cognition and perception) in the individual (McLuhan 1972) on the one hand, and as a basic cause for transformation of social institution and organisation (Goody and Watt 1963; Goody 1968) on the other hand. In fact, the ethnography of literacy implicitly carries with it the perspective, what literacy does for an individual as a self and for a society as an institution. Quite distinct from this is the viewpoint of those who are involved with the literacy curriculum. The educational perspective is more concerned with the question, what individuals can do with literacy. It is based primarily on the untested convictions of planners that (a) literacy invariably leads to improved social and economic status and (b) literacy is the prerequisite of functional education. Policy framers for literacy education have thus restricted its semantics more centrally to the minimum competency movement. They have tried to apply the term to a wide range of skills, within which an attempt has been made to identify the following four levels of performance: (1) nominal literacy, (2) minimal literacy, (3) functional literacy, and (4) full literacy (Elson 1967). However, scholars engaged with literacy education have recently rejected such a naive classification primarily on the basis that it neither reflects the processes involved in literacy education nor corresponds to the social functions of reading and writing. Before we discuss what kinds of influence communication setting has over literacy achievement and to what extent choice of language and language style exercises its control over literacy, it is necessary that we grasp the semantics of literacy through our understanding of two pairs of concepts — literacy versus nonliteracy and illiterate versus uneducated.

Nonliteracy is a condition of a society where writing has neither been able to evolve sufficient conditions for its meaningful usage nor has it been able to generate a value for literate culture with a special status that marginalizes those who are conditioned to the life-style of an esoteric oral culture. *Illiteracy*, on the other hand, is a condition of "an individual or a group that has failed to master the generally accepted skills of the culture and is thus cut off from the cultural heritage of contemporaries" (Finnegan 1972). It is true that in an advanced society literacy takes a social form in the emergence of occupations which require reading and writing skills for their operational implementation. In such a context those who are deprived of literacy skills can be labelled as illiterates. However, studies of certain societies and educational movements have also shown that educational gains can be made in certain situations even without proficiency in literacy skills. For example, charity schools in London in the eighteenth century provided free educational facilities, but their main emphasis was on social discipline and religious education; and, as pointed out by Marshall (1926) and Jones (1938), the three Rs — reading, writing, and arithmetic — were rarely pursued. Similarly, Meggitt (1968) has shown that during the millenarian movements, in New Guinea and Melanesia, parents on a large scale withdrew their children from the literacy campaign. This happened when parents realized that their economic status could not be improved even after their sons achieved proficiency in literacy skills. Given the milieu in which a common Indian villager performs his day-to-day activities and provides for the infrastructure that supports rural poverty, one would like to ask whether the condition of a villager as an individual or a social worker attests nonliteracy or illiteracy.

Education has been defined by UNESCO as "organized and sustained communication designed to bring about learning" (UNESCO 1976). An educated person is one who possesses a critical mind, organised knowledge, and skilled ability resulting from his learning. Thus, learning to be educated is not merely the memory of facts but rather the acquisition of knowledge and organisation of experience helpful to the learner in adjusting and controling the environment. In this broader perspective of the concept, one may say that, in our society, we can find in good numbers "literate uneducated" as well as "illiterate educated". It needs no emphasis that an average illiterate Indian is not necessarily uneducated. We have great many instances of great saints of the type of Kabirdas, Ravidas, etc., who were acknowledged educators and social reformers of their time in spite of never having come in contact with paper and ink.

This raises two types of fundamental questions.

(a) What is the nature of the channel of communication which brings about learning in illiterate but educated Indians? What mode of education do these illiterate educands exploit for their accomplished achievements? What gains will these people have after acquiring an ability to use their language in a written medium? These queries cannot satisfactorily be answered unless we develop a set of paradigms which explore the link between literacy and social organization, and further, between literacy and education.

(b) What is the nature and functioning of our education system, running from primary school to university, which produces graduates who master the skill of reading and writing and yet are unable to bring about the condition for learning through the use of the printed page as a means of communication. It is reported by Rozin and Gleitman (1977) that more than 10 per cent of American adults are "functionally illiterate". Our own study shows that no less than 46 per cent of community health workers (CHW) in India read below the expected fourth-grade level (Srivastava 1978b). No less than 70 per cent of them showed instances of semilingualism. It is no less interesting to explore the factors which can be considered responsible for creating "semilingualism" and "functional illiteracy". These questions cannot satisfactorily be answered unless we develop a set of paradigms which explore the links between literacy and language use, and further, between literacy and its ethnographic effects.

The fact must not be lost sight of that literacy not only involves many variables but also entails many aspects of its realization. It is necessary for our discussion that at least its following three aspects be distinguished:

(i) *Orientational* (mathemagenic factors): the ability to control the visual (graphic) medium (reading and writing) of a language. Speech is acquired in response to a biologically endowed language faculty. Our organs of acoustic encoding and decoding are evolutionarily adapted to discharge their function of articulation and auditory perception (Lenneberg 1967, Lieberman 1977). The same is not true with the organs involved in reading. In fact, "reading is a comparatively new and arbitrary human ability for which specific biological adaptations do not, so far as we know, exist .... The problem with reading is not a visual perception problem; the problem is rather that the eye is not biologically adapted to language" (Gleitman and Rozin 1977:3). The orientational aspect of literacy is concerned with all those visual and manual modalities which are implicated in the difficulty of learning to read and write. It is concerned with our skill called "decoding" writing into speech and "encoding" speech into writing.

(ii) *Operational* (performance factors): the ability to use a language in a written medium. This has much wider implications for literacy. Literacy is not merely "sounding our" of words or sentences; it is the skill of reading with understanding and comprehension. We found too much of mismatch between scores obtained from oral and written comprehension tests we designed for CHWs (Srivastava 1978b). This aspect is also concerned with the control of the variant of a language which is institutionally employed in the ecological setting of writing.

(iii) *Functional* (psychosociological factors): the ability to employ the written language as an instrument for one's psychological remake of "phonetic culture" for the eulogy of intuition and imagination and as a tool for radical reorientation of social life and culture. It is in this context that McLuhan declared that "phonetic literacy" as has penetrated in oral-aural communities of China and India has altered very little their world of sound. According to him, "even Russia is still profoundly oral in bias. Only gradually does literacy alter substructures of language and sensibility" (McLuhan 1962:21).

I am concerned in this paper mainly with the operational aspect of literacy. This aspect has much wider implications, when language is viewed as a code, as it is concerned not only with the control of the medium of communication but also with the control of the variant of a language which is institutionally employed in the ecological setting of writing. In a multilingual setting like ours literacy parameters implicate factors such as language or style choices. It is not difficult to see the reason why the highest rate of illiteracy in India exists in the Hindi-speaking region extending from Rajasthan to Bihar and in a Telugu-speaking State, i.e., Andhra Pradesh. It is in this region that the written standard variety of a language is far removed in grammar and vocabulary from the local vernacular and home variant of the language. For example, the Hindi-speaking region shows a diglossic situation of the type dialect versus language, while the Telugu speech community is characterized by diglossia of Granthika style (a literary standard) and Vyavaharika style (a colloquial standard). De Silva (1976) has shown full evidence of how tensions that diglossia create seem to be damaging in the pursuit of literacy goals.

Concerned literature on literacy raises two conflicting claims related to its operational efficiency:

(a)   Literacy as a skill is most effectively achieved in the mothertongue (as literacy generally presupposes articulacy), and

(b)   Literacy as a function is most effectively achieved in the language (of wider communication) which has its semantic and social setting of esoteric written culture.

It is obvious that the former defines literacy as an extension of the functional potential of language with regard to the written mode of transmission and makes a plea for *vernacular literacy*. This approach does not propose knowledge of the standard variant of a language as a precondition for initiating literacy. Rather, acquisition of the standard language is considered a natural consequence of the literacy process in action. The latter point of view accepts literacy as a call for participation of the socially deprived and economically disadvantaged illiterate masses into the heritage of written culture. This approach is conditioned by people's idealization of language and tends to promote *standard language* literacy.

These two different orientations make two conflicting demands on the language used in literacy programmes, especially in the context of our multilingual setting. In India, mothertongues (MTs) are generally neither languages of wider communication nor are they employed in the ecological setting to which writing is contextually appropriate. As there are some MTs which have no writing system of their own and some, though written, have relatively lower status and restricted function, we find in our educational programmes cases where literacy is initiated through a language which is not the learners' own language.

There are many instances and several types of situations in India in which literacy skills are being initiated through a second language. The first situation is basically concerned with tribal or minority (nonliterate) language speakers. Some of the other situations can be exemplified by literacy patterns from Hindi regions. Literacy here is initiated through primers written in "Standard Hindi" at the cost of linguistically distinct dialects in which learners have exclusive communicative proficiency. Another instance of initiating literacy in the second language can be seen in English-medium schools. In spite of the fact that learners are brought up in the environment of written regional language at home and in society, they are first imparted literacy in English (Srivastava 1978a).

Despite the fact that students are brought up in the environment of their mother-tongue (with no oral competence in Standard Hindi in the village setting), they are made to acquire literacy skills in Hindi. It is a similar case with English-medium schools. Students are imparted literacy skills in English – a language in which their "capacity as well as opportunity for use is extremely limited when compared to the native speakers of English" (Sah 1978). The result is that we come across students who do not know either of the two languages properly. In addition to this semilingualism, the promotion of standard language literacy in our multilingual and pluricultural society is producing a subtractive type of bilingualism for minority populations in a major way.

In order to find out how and to what extent standard language literacy policy is downgrading the mother dialect and other language styles actually employed in real-life situations, an attitude test was designed and administered to two sets of school children of Varanasi District.

Set I: Village setting; Hindi medium school with English as a compulsory subject; Class X; number of informants – 25.

Set II: Urban setting; English medium school with Hindi as a compulsory subject; Class X; number of informants – 25.

Students were asked to rank in order of their preference selected passages specially written in the following five styles: (i) Hindi, (ii) English, (iii) Dialect (Bhojpuri), (iv) Dialect mixed Hindi, and (v) English mixed Hindi. The ranking divided into three categories – High (H), Moderate (M) and Low (L) – is shown below:

Language: Style	Village Setting (Hindi Medium School with English as a compulsory subject)			Urban Setting (English Medium School with Hindi as a compulsory subject)		
	H	M	L	H	M	L
Hindi	87.12	12.88	00.00	79.74	20.20	00.00
English	48.02	51.98	00.00	81.00	19.00	00.00
Dialect	05.45	10.14	84.41	00.00	00.00	100.00
Dialect mixed Hindi	28.14	11.98	60.88	08.15	02.00	89.85
English mixed Hindi	00.00	08.28	91.72	14.00	22.00	64.00

The ranking is divided into three categories:

High   (H) – first and second preferences
Moderate (M) – third preference
Low   (L) – fourth and fifth preferences

Linguistic Attitude Scores

The following two inferences can be drawn from the attitude scores of the two groups:

(i)   Both groups accord high ranking to Hindi and English.
(ii) Both groups accord a very low ranking to dialect and code-mixed variety of Hindi.

This simply shows how schools are functioning as a selective instrument for perpetuating middle-class ethnocentric norms of language usage in which those linguistic codes/styles are stigmatized which are instrumental for learning through experience. Dialect in a village setting is a language of experience, and code-mixing is a real phenomenon of day-to-day verbal activity. Still, literacy skills are imparted through a puritan viewpoint of language which helps generate semilingualism. If we define "reading as the skill of extracting meaning from print to the same degree that one extracts it from the sound stream" (Gleitman and Rozin 1977:7), our study shows that our education system gradually increases in the learner the original gap between oral and written comprehension (Srivastava 1978b).

The present-day practice of initiating literacy in the second language, first of all, violates the operational efficiency condition that literacy is most effectively achieved in MT and, secondly, leaves certain negatively marked effects on the language and social organization. Some of these effects are as follows:

it leaves many learners at the level of semi-literacy,
creates intellectual imbalances between standard language literacy and mass illiteracy,
downgrades the learners' mother-tongue,
interferes with the channel for cross-cultural communication that could serve as a bridge between oral culture and written culture, and
it generates disharmonious relationships between functions of literacy (i.e. what literacy does for learners) and uses of literacy (i.e. what learners do with literacy skills).

But the higher preferential attitude scores accorded to Hindi and English by the two groups of informants belonging to schools in rural and urban settings clearly indicate what the learners want to achieve in their terminal or target behavior. It is quite obvious that learners — whether they belong to rural areas or urban centres — prefer to acquire literacy skills in languages and styles which are controlled by elitist structures. Control of the "written standard" will naturally have a higher social value because it becomes a symbol of prestige and power. Literacy becomes sociologically functional when it is achieved in the language which has its significance and functionality in the contextual setting of written culture. This goal is best achieved by taking recourse to standard language literacy instead of vernacular literacy. However, a crucial point that is often missed in setting the literacy goal is the process by which it can best be achieved. It is our contention that the initial stage of literacy is no less important than its terminal stage and that, in our multilingual setting, the two stages may not opt for the same language and/or style.

The learner in the initial stage of literacy education seems to operate most efficiently in the language of the home and the peer group. Literacy programmes thus must initially draw their linguistic resources from the dialect/ vernacular and thereafter make a gradual transfer to the preferred terminal behaviour, i.e., standard and standardized languages. If we lose sight of this distinction between the initial stage of literacy and its terminal stage, we are likely to foster the growth of either semilingualism or the subtractive type of bilingualism. An example is in order here. We do have dialect-based creative literature (Suradasa and Biharidasa in Braj, Jayasi and Tulasidasa in Avadhi, Vidyapati in Maithili, etc.) as part of our formal education curriculum both at the school and the university stages. The study of this literature is introduced after the learners have gained a command of the standard variety. It has often been observed that learners demonstrate a low level of competence while switching over from the standard variety to the dialect. The case is similar with learners studying in the English-medium schools where they would switch from English to Hindi. It has been observed that this switch-over is characterized by a low level of competence in both languages. Our proposal will entail reading initiation in the vernacular — say Awadhi, Braj, Maithili, etc. — making the learning of the standard language a concomitant affair of reading and writing activities, a reversal of what the process has been in our formal system of education.

As pointed out elsewhere (Srivastava 1979), we have to evolve our own literacy model to yield the best result in our multilingual and pluricultural setting. Our proposed model suggests initiating literacy in the language/ style in which educands have oral competence and then transfer it, if necessary, to the code recognized as the medium of instruction in our formal educational system. The advantage of this Vernacular-cum-Transfer Literacy Model lies in the fact that it will neither generate pressure on educands for learning two skills at a time — literacy skill (i.e., reading and writing) as well as articulacy skill (i.e., speaking and listening) in a (standard) language (which educands happen not to know) - nor will it stigmatize the educands' (mother) dialect.

References

DeSilva, M.W.S. 1976. *Diglossia and Literacy,* Mysore: CIIL.

Elson, D.G. 1967. *Report of Some Observations on Literacy Programmes in India.* Indian University.

Finnegan, R. 1972. Literacy versus Non-literacy: The Great Divide. In: Robin Horton and Ruth Finnegan, eds. *Modes of Thought.* London: Faber and Faber.

Gleitman, L.R. and Rozin, P. 1977. The Structure and Acquisition of Reading I: Relations between Orthographies and the Structure of Language. In Arthur S. Reber and Don L. Scarborough, eds. *Toward a Psychology of Reading* (1–53). New Jersey: L.E. Associates.

Goody, J., ed. 1968. *Literacy in Traditional Societies.* Cambridge: Cambridge University Press.

Goody, J. and Watt, I.P. 1963. The Consequences of Literacy. *Comparative Studies in History and Society* 5. 304–345.

Jones, M.G. 1938. *The Charity School Movement.* Cambridge.

Lenneberg, E. 1967. *Biological foundations of language.* New York: John Wiley & Sons.

Lieberman, P. 1977. *Speech Physiology and Acoustic Phonetics: An Introduction.* New York: Macmillan.

Marshall, D. 1926. *The English Poor in the Eighteenth Century.* London.

McLuhan, M. 1962. *The Gutenberg Galaxy: The Making of Typographic Man.* London: Routledge.

Meggitt, M. 1968. Uses of Literacy in New Guinea and Melanesia. In: J. Goody ed. *Literacy in Traditional Societies.* Cambridge: Cambridge University Press.

Rozin, P. and Gleitman, L.R. 1977. The Structure and Acquisition of Reading II: The Reading Process and the Acquisition of the Alphabetic Principle. In Arthur S. Reber and Don L. Scarborough, eds. *Toward a Psychology of Reading* (55–141). New Jersey: L.E. Associates.

Sah, P.F. 1978. Literacy, Language Use and Modes of Thought. *Language Forum* 4. 31–44.

Srivastava, R.N. 1978a. Literacy, Language Use and Culture. *Language Forum* 4, 1–21.

– 1978b. Evaluating Communicability in Village Settings. UNICEF Delhi.

– 1979. Literacy as a Communication Skill. *Indian Journal of Adult Education* 40. 1–14.

UNESCO 1976. *International Standard Classification of Education.* Division of Statistics on Education.

Literacy education for minorities:
A case study from India

R. N. SRIVASTAVA, *UNIVERSITY OF DELHI*

Before I present my brief statement on the problems raised by Florian Coulmas, let me throw some light on the multidimensional complexity which multilingual, multiethnic, and multicultural India as a whole offers with respect to literacy education for its linguistic minorities.

Administrative and Population Statistics

The Indian Union at present consists of 22 States and 9 Union territories with a population of approximately 600 million. For administrative convenience, the states and Union territories are divided into 360 districts of varying size and population.

It is to be noted that the question of reorganization of the states of the Indian Union on a linguistic basis led to the appointment of the States Reorganization Commission on 29 December 1953. Based on the Report of the Commission, a number of unilingual states were formed in the year 1956. The main motivating force behind this scheme of redistribution of state territories has been the idea of reducing the number of linguistic minorities by bringing people together who speak a common language.

But the reorganization of states on a linguistic basis could not solve all the problems of linguistic minorities. In 1956 there were only 16 states in India, whereas now we find 22 states and 9 Union territories. The process of bifurcation of states has some relevance for the study of the nature of minorities. Maharashtra was bifurcated in 1960 into two states because of the two prominent speech communities — Gujarati and Marathi, and in 1966 Punjab was divided into Punjabi Suma and Haryana because of the conflict between two ethnic groups — Hindu and Sikh, the former adhering to Hindi and the latter to the Punjabi language. It is to be noted that Sikhs constitute the third major religious minority community in India with 10,378,796 persons, i.e., 1.89 % of the total Indian population (Table I).

TABLE 1: Major Religious Communities of India

COMMUNITIES	1961	1971
I. Hindus	83.50 %	82.72 %
II. (i) Muslims	10.70 %	11.21 %
(ii) Christians	2.44 %	2.60 %
(iii) Sikhs	1.79 %	1.89 %

Sikhs are primarily concentrated in Punjab, but even there they were in a minority, as is evident from the 1961 census statistics. They were in fact 33.33 % of the total population of the state. After the reorganization, the Sikh population in Punjab rose to 60.22 %, as is revealed by the 1971 census. Sikhs as a religious group now became the dominant majority. The case has been similar with respect to the Punjabi and Hindi languages. Table 2 speaks of this fact for itself.

TABLE 2: Hindi – Punjabi in the Punjab

1961		1971	
Hindi	Punjabi	Hindi	Punjabi
55.6 %	41.1 %	20.01 %	79.49 %

What was in 1961 a "minority" language in the Punjab state became a "majority" in 1971 and vice-versa so far as Hindi and Punjabi languages are concerned. This type of situation happened wherever the redistribution of state territories took place. This simply showed that linguistic reorganization of states in itself cannot solve all the problems of linguistic minorities, simply because different states are basically multilingual and pluricultural complexes. This can be seen through our Table 3, which shows that no state in India has fewer than 12 mothertongues; in fact, the mothertongues ranges from 12 to 410.

TABLE 3: Statewise distribution of languages

Name of the State/ Territory	No. of Indian mother tongues spoken	No. of foreign mother tongues spoken	Total
Andhra Pradesh	186	24	210
Assam	162	30	192
Bihar	121	32	153
Gujrat	106	32	138
Jammu & Kashmir	90	13	103
Kerala	69	41	110
Madhya Pradesh	233	25	258
Madras	100	59	159
Maharashtra	410	53	463
Mysore	128	42	170
Nagaland	89	6	95
Orissa	50	8	58
Punjab	135	26	161
Rajasthan	78	11	89
Uttar Pradesh	117	25	142
West Bengal	236	37	273
Delhi	92	49	141
Himachal Pradesh	203	7	210
Goa, Daman and Diu	15	13	28
Pondichery	36	19	55
Dadara & Nagar Haveli	23	3	26
L.M. & Islands	12	2	14
A. & N. Islands	65	8	73
Manipur	82	5	87
Tripura	107	5	112
NEFA	162	6	168

(Source: Census of India – 1961)

It is to be emphasized that the reorganization of linguistic states as political and administrative units was based on the principle of reducing the conflict between the major minority language speakers of India. But in the process, it gave a new dimension of conflict and tensions to different minority speech communities which earlier enjoyed peaceful coexistence. This is aptly reflected in the First Report of the Commissioner for Linguistic Minorities, which states: "The division of States on linguistic basis has given rise to the inevitable result that the regional language should gain prominence and should in course of time become the official language of the State. The other languages which are the mother-tongue of the minority communities living in the State, naturally do not get equal prominence or status. The result is that those whose mother-tongue is the minority language have not only a sentimental grievance but certain practical difficulties and inconveniences from which they suffer."

Thus we find that different states of India might have been declared uni- or bilingual for political exigencies or administrative convenience, but basically each of them is a multilingual and polyethnic complex entity. Consequently, even if the state boundaries were drawn rigidly on the principle of uni- or bilingual states, the problem of linguistic minorities would remain unsolved.

Language Profile of India and the Status of Linguistic Minorities

With 600 million population, 1652 mother-tongues, 67 educational languages, and 10 major writing systems, India is obviously the finest but most complicated laboratory for social research. Some of its salient features related to language profile are given below:

(i)   Different vernaculars of India fall under four families: Indo-Aryan, Dravidian, Austro-Asiatic, and Sino-Tibetan.
(ii)   The linguistic scene in India is dominated by two family groups with a population covering 97.7 % of its total population.
(iii)   Fifteen major languages (i.e., languages specified in the VIII Schedule of the Indian Constitution) cover 88 % of the speakers of the total population.
(iv)   The two official languages of the Union – Hindi (primary) and English (associate) – together cover more than half of the entire bilingual population.
(v)   There are only 240 MTs (i.e. 12 %) which have ten thousand and more speakers; MTs having less than a thousand speakers are 1248 in number (i.e. 75 %). (This indicates that numerous dialects and pockets of tribal inhabitants exist with distinct identities and ethnic backgrounds and that they have not been integrated to form a larger superordinate group.)

We all know that, underlying language policy, there remain always the wider principles of national policy. The national policy recommended the following measures:

(a)   for strengthening the Constitutional safeguards for linguistic minorities,
(b)   for promoting regional languages (mentioned in the VIII Schedule) to official status, and
(c)   for integrating India through two pan-Indian languages – Hindi (as a primary official language) and English (as an associate official language).

These measures led our national language policy makers to evolve the *Three Language Formula*. It stipulated the following language subjects for teaching at the school stage of our education:

(i)   the regional language and mother tongue when the latter is different from the regional language;
(ii)   Hindi or, in Hindi-speaking areas, another Indian language; and
(iii)   English or any other modern European language.

There are two specific articles (Art. 29 and 30) in the Constitution which safeguard the rights and interests of minority communities. These articles are intended to protect the minorities from any discrimination against them on grounds of religion, race, caste, or language. All minorities were given the right to conserve their language, script, and culture. In one of its judgements, the Supreme Court ruled that the right to conserve includes the right of the citizens "to agitate for the protection of the language" (Jagat Singh Vs Pratap Singh AIR 1965 SC 183).

The States Reorganization Commission soon realized that languages of minority groups are commonly not among the languages mentioned in the VIII Schedule to the Constitution. And, it recommended certain measures to promote the cause of linguistic minorities. Consequently, Articles 350A and 350B were added to the Constitution. According to Art. 350A, states are directed to provide adequate facilities for instruction in the MT at the primary stage of education to children belonging to linguistic minority groups. Art. 350B empowered the president to appoint a special officer for linguistic minorities who will investigate all matters relating to the safeguards provided for linguistic minorities under our Constitution.

To the question: are there any conflicts between the rights of ethnic and linguistic minorities to use and preserve their language and the desire of centralized states to establish a national language as a universal means of communication and administration, the answer for India is both No and Yes. The answer is partly No because India in principle is committed to the principle of integration rather than forced assimilation or segregation. Integration helps different ethnic and linguistic groups maintain their identity in some respect but make them merge into a superordinate group in some other respects. The Three Language Formula was meant to integrate the society through educational measures by this principle of integration.

The answer to the above-raised question is also partly Yes because in the process of achieving its ideal, i.e., unity in diversity, India gave to certain languages the role of dominant language. A *dominant* language is one which gets impregnated with the power which blocks the upward social mobility of the members of other speech groups. If we look at the status of English in India, we find that it enjoys the administrative privileges and sociopolitical power in society *par excellence*. English as a dominant minority (elite) language is the first and foremost cause for the disequilibrium of our multilingual society. The official status of Hindi at the Centre and the 13 other major regional languages at the level of states also play the role of dominant languages. It is worth noting that in pre-independent India, Hindi was the most potent means of unification and integration. It was the voice of protest against the imperialist power, a vehicular language for mass upsurge and a cultivator of new values free from class and creed. It was a language for mass participation. Soon after it became a "dominant" language, it got looked upon by a section of the people as a symbol of communalism and language chauvinism, and, over and above, a linguistic instrument of oppression of minority languages. What is true of Hindi is true for the dominant languages as well.

Literacy and Linguistic Minorities

We have defined *literacy* as an extension of the functional potential of a language with regard to the written mode of transmission involving writing and reading skills. However, one has to differentiate between the following three aspects of literacy:

(a) Literacy as a control of the visual (graphic) *medium* of a language (i.e. reading and writing skills),
(b) literacy as an ability to *use a language* in a written medium, and
(c) literacy as a tool to achieve certain sociocultural ends.

These three aspects of literacy are vital for our understanding of the functionality and relevance of literacy. The first aspect confines the scope of literacy merely to linguistic skills, while the third aspect defines literacy as a call for participation of the socially deprived and economically disadvantaged illiterate masses into the heritage of written culture.

It goes without saying that our nation is confronted with a serious problem of illiteracy. It is true that, due to our launching of massive adult education programmes, the percentage of literacy over the years has improved. But it is equally true that, in our country, the population growth is out of proportion to availability of literacy facilities. Consequently, although the literacy rate increased from 19.26 percent in 1951 to 34.08 percent in 1971, the total number of illiterates also increased from 173.9 to 209.5 millions. This is evident from Table 4.

TABLE 4: Percentage Literacy (age-group above 14 Yrs)

YEAR	% OF LITERACY	NUMBER OF ILLITERATES (IN MILLIONS)
1951	19.26	173.9
1961	27.76	187.0
1971	34.08	209.5

This table hides more than it reveals. It conceals the fact that literates in rural areas are far fewer in number than in urban areas, and that females on the whole are less literate than males. This is evident from Table 5 (which is based on the 1971 Census).

TABLE 5: Literacy in Urban & Rural

	MALE			FEMALE		
	Population	Literates	%	Population	Literates	%
Urban	58,522,821	36,021,828	61.55	50,264,261	21,067,701	41.91
Rural	224,729,393	75,889,172	33.77	213,851,451	27,631,490	12.92

The following table (Table 6) reveals literacy percentages among the scheduled tribe population in 1971.

TABLE 6: Literacy among Tribals

TOTAL TRIBE POPULATION		LITERATES AMONG SCHEDULED TRIBE POPULATION	
		Number	%
	38,015,162	4,296,779	11.30
Male	19,181,450	3,382,567	17.63
Female	18,833,712	914,212	4.85

According to the 1971 Census, the scheduled tribe population comprises about 6.94 % of the total population of India. The overall literacy level among tribals is merely 11.30 %. The literacy rate varies from almost zero (among Dorlas in Madhya Pradesh) to 60 % (among Khasi in the north-east) amongst the tribals.

If we consider that Scheduled Castes (SC) and Scheduled Tribes (ST) are two major categories of people who constitute in a major way economically disadvantaged minority groups in India, then it is interesting to see their literacy percentage and its decennial variation in the context of the overall literacy percentage of India. This is shown in Table 7.

Literacy is recognized by India as a desirable goal for everyone. But the question is how to achieve this goal for 450 tribes having no fewer than 294 classified MTs? The first big question is about the choice of language and script for the functionality of literacy. Experts on literacy raise two conflicting claims related to its operational efficiency:

TABLE 7: Literacy Percentage: Overall and in Minority Groups

Year	All India 1	S C 2	S T 3	Average of 2 & 3
1961	24.04	10.27	8.54	9.45
1971	29.35	14.71	11.29	13.00

(a) Literacy as a skill is most effectively achieved in MT (as literacy generally presupposes articulacy). This I would like to call *Vernacular Literacy.*

(b) Literacy as a function is most effectively achieved in the language (of wider communication) which has the semantic and social setting of esoteric written culture. This I would prefer to label *Standard Language Literacy.*

These two different orientations make two conflicting demands on the language used in literacy programmes, especially in the context of our multilingual setting. I have discussed them in detail in my paper "Consequences of Initiating Literacy in the Second Language" (pp. 29ff. above). Our proposed model suggests the following:

(1) Initiate literacy in the language style in which illiterates have oral competence and then transfer it, if necessary, to the language recognized as the medium of instruction in the formal educational system of the region.

(2) If the tribal language has to be given a writing system, select the script of the regional state language (rather than devise a new script); however, if the minority community has a strongly negative attitude towards the script of the regional language, Devnagari may be used as it is this script which, in Art. 343 (1) of the Indian Constitution, has been recognized for the Union's official language. This proposal implies that a tribal language with a written tradition should not be forced to discontinue the use of its own script.

In modifying a script to serve efficiently a new language, a number of linguistic as well as extralinguistic factors have to be taken into consideration. The following steps have to be taken in this direction:

(a) Establish the phonemic inventory of the target language;

(b) identify the need for new symbols for phonemes which are missing from the source language;

(c) provide the necessary additional symbols (which should be in character close to the nature and style of the selected writing system).

There are extralinguistic factors which may outweigh linguistic considerations; for example, tones in AO Naga are phonemic. However, when diacritic marks for tones were provided in the writing system (AO uses Roman Script), native users rejected them on the grounds that it makes the system cumbersome.

The problem of minority languages in the overall linguistic problems of our time

S. TAKDIR ALISJAHBANA, *UNIVERSITAS NASIONAL, JAKARTA*

The language problem is more than just the problem of the expression of human thought in sound or written symbols which gives man an extensive means of communication. Language is involved in the totality of the culture of a society and its people. Every word represents a concept in that culture. Thus the totality of the vocabulary of a language realizes the totality of the concepts of that culture – concepts which are related to each other in an interlocked structure, expressing the value configuration of that culture with its richness of feelings, iideas, and ambitions. Therefore we can say that every language is the complete expression of the life or, as is very often said, "the soul" of the people. This is the reason why the language problem is permeated with so much emotion, sentiment, or even fanatism, as we witness in the language conflicts in India, Sri Lanka, and many young African States, or even in the attitude of the minorities in many advanced countries such as that of the Basques in Spain.

The problem of national languages and linguistic minorities has especially arisen with the creation of the new national states in Asia and Africa after the Second World War. The colonial territories of the European powers which became independent, were very often populated by various peoples and tribes, each with their own language and culture which in many ways differed from each other, so that no adequate communication could and can take place between the different groups. In the colonial epoch the dominant language for inter-group communication was the language of the colonial power.

Indonesia is a good example. In the Indonesian archipelago, which consists of thousands of islands, about six hundred languages and dialects are spoken, the largest of which, such as the Javanese languages, are spoken by fifty million people, while some of the other languages are spoken by only a few hundred thousand people.

During the colonial period the dominant language was, of course, Dutch. Second place was taken by the Malay language which was the lingua franca in Southeast Asia for more than a thousand years.

Indonesia was in a favorable situation, since its youth discovered very early that the Indonesian people would only be successful in their struggle against the Dutch colonial power if they could be united into a single social and cultural, and especially political, force. That was the decisive meaning of the oath of the youth of Indonesia in 1928 for *one country, one nation* and *one language*, all called Indonesia. It is of course strange that the Javanese population, consisting of about fifty million people, and the Sundanese of twenty five million gave up their languages in favor of the Indonesian national language, which was for them a foreign language. Their decision shows us how strong their longing for independence and freedom was: that they even gave up their own language.

There are of course many sociocultural factors which could influence a group of people to neglect their own language for the acceptance of another more or less foreign language. The Javanese, for example, preferred Malay to their own language as the national language of Indonesia because there are various drawbacks inherent in the Javanese language, when facing the modern sociocultural situation which the Javanese people have accepted. The Javanese language is a very complicated language, consisting of three or more layers, each with its own vocabulary. An older Javanese uses another vocabulary when he addresses a younger person than the younger one who speaks to him. So does a Javanese of a higher standing, when addressing a Javanese of lower standing. This special characteristic of the Javanese language is the result of the feudal past of the Javanese people, which in one way or another has been influenced by Indian caste stratification. In any case the language is not democratic and does not appeal to the younger generation which has been educated in the democratic atmosphere of Dutch schools.

Another important factor is that the island of Java is the most populated island of the Indonesian archipelago with relatively limited resources; the Javanese people need the extensive space and resources of the other, rather thinly populated islands, the area of which is seven times that of Java, for its further developments.

Thus, according to the curriculum of the primary school in Indonesia today, its pupils have to learn and utilize the Indonesian language from the first year on. If necessary, the teacher is allowed to use the local language, which helps him in his communication with his pupils. The Javanese language is a subject only during the full six years of primary school education.

In this context it is interesting to mention that the Javanese language is culturally the most highly developed language of Indonesia with a rich religious and philosophical literature. Some writers have deplored the fact that this rich and highly developed language cannot be transformed into a fullfledged modern language. The same is of course true for the Sundanese language, spoken by about twenty-five million people. I am not speaking here about the smaller languages in Indonesia, which, of course, have more and more retreated to the background and some of which will gradually disappear. Through the spread of education, which is planned to be compulsory in a few years, the Indonesian language will soon be spoken and understood by the whole population of Indonesia.

But what is the alternative for such large and important languages as the Javanese and the Sundanese languages? It is clear that these languages are experiencing a decline, since all laws and official pronouncements, all newspapers, magazines and books, all education from the primary school until the university are in the Indonesian language.

It is obvious that the Javanese as well as the Sundanese languages can only come to full development if they become the language for the entire formal education from the primary school until the university and for the whole modern social and cultural life of the Javanese and Sundanese people, which expresses itself in the language. Considering the number of Javanese- and Sundanese-speaking people, both languages could easily be developed into a modern language like Dutch in the Netherlands, the Danish language in Denmark, etc. But in this phase of Indonesian social, cultural, and especially political life, which emphasizes the unity of the country and its people, such a development is out of the question. On the contrary, the influence of the Indonesian language on both languages is very strong, especially in relation to the vocabulary and expressions, which deal with the modern world and the overall Indonesian cultural life. There is a converging tendency in both languages toward the Indonesian language. A remarkable phenomenon shows that during the last decade Javanese and Sundanese writers have dominated the Indonesian literary scene, while the literature of the Javanese and the Sundanese language is unable to develop adequately.

This Indonesian language situation, with such large languages as Javanese and Sundanese being dominated or pushed aside by the national language which is basically Malay without any meaningful resistance from these languages, is quite an exception in our time. We hear about so many conflicts concerning the language scene in the new national states, such as, India, Pakistan, Sri Lanka, Malaysia, Singapore, and especially in Africa. But even in some modern European countries there are still quarrels concerning the choice of an official language, such as the claim of the Basque minority in Spain for the recognition of their language as one of the official languages of the country.

What are the problems if, in a country, a minority or minorities are struggling for the recognition of their languages? In the most extreme cases such movements usually go hand in hand with separatism, i.e., movements for independence or a certain degree of autonomy, i.e., to form a new nation or an autonomous part of the country with its own language and cultural identity. That is the case with the Armenian people in Turkey and Russia, or with the Kurds in Iran, Iraq, and Turkey, and maybe also with some linguistic groups in India, Pakistan, and Sri Lanka. In these cases the people involved intend to continue to live their own lives in the modern world culturally and languagewise. The language should then become modernized, in order to become eventually a modern language of its own, i.e., the language of administration and law, the medium of instruction from primary school to university, etc. This is of course not an easy task, because a host of new problems emerge which can only be faced if the language community is large, vital, and rich enough to cope with it. In order to develop a language into a modern one, many problems have to be solved. The development of a language from a premodern language into a modern one — i.e., into a vehicle of modern science and technology — requires a complex and time-consuming effort to create thousands of modern terms and to provide the language with books and other reading materials. I can say that until now none of the languages of the new nations has achieved this aim satisfactorily, neither the Hindi language of India, the Urdu of Pakistan, nor the Mandarin of China or the Indonesian language of Indonesia. The great exception is, of course, the language of Japan, which started its modernization process in the Meiji era and during a period of less than a century has translated nearly any relevant book from any language into Japanese. After World War II alone, more than 150,000 books were translated into Japanese.

Some fifty years ago there was a group of educators and linguists who were of the opinion that the development of a child's mind requires that teaching during the first school years should take place in the mother tongue of the child. If a child would start too early to think in a foreign language, its intellectual capacity would be harmed in its further growth. This theory came up in Indonesia during the colonial period, when the Indonesian parents made all efforts to get their children accepted in Dutch schools, where all the teaching took place in the Dutch language. Dr. Nieuwenhuis, a well-known language educator in the Dutch Indies of those days, introduced the so-called *Schakelschool*, i.e., a school type which in a period of three years brought the children from the five-year primary schools, where the medium of instruction was the native language such as Malay, Javanese, Sundanese, etc., to the same level as the children who had their education for seven years entirely in the Dutch language.

There was indeed a great confusion in the understanding between the colonial government and the native population. The first wanted to promote primary school education in the native tongue for the benefit of the intellectual development of the native child, while on the other hand the Indonesians wanted eagerly to learn the Dutch language as early as possible, in order to get access in the most direct way to modern culture with its progress in science and technology.

The mistrust on the Indonesian side even increased when the Dutch colonial government attempted to promote the use of the smaller regional languages such as the Minangkabau and the Aceh language in the primary school. From the Indonesian side this effort was considered as an attempt of the Dutch colonial power policy of *divide et impera* to undermine the growing influence of the Indonesian national language.

Another aspect of the problems involved in the languages of minorities is their cultural value, not only for the minorities involved but also for the whole of humankind. We have said before that language is the most complete expression of a culture, so that the defence of a language very often is synonymous with the defence of a culture or at least certain traits or characteristics of it. This is of course a very important problem of Indonesia today, since the Javanese, Sundanese, Balinese and still many other smaller languages represent the very rich core of the Indonesian traditional culture, especially in the arts. This is of course not a problem in the plastic arts, nor in music and dance, which do not make use of language. It is however quite different in the famous Javanese, Balinese, and Sundanese dramas, especially in the performing arts of the *wayang*, the mythologies, the songs, folklores, and other narratives, in which language forms the most important element. Efforts have been made, not unsuccessfully, to give these performances in the national language, in order to make them available to a larger public. But it is clear that such performances are in many ways unsatisfactory for the native speaker, who was used to hearing these performances in his or her own native tongue. Thus the Indonesian Government established regional radio and TV centers, which at certain times broadcast their own programmes for the need of the region and very often also in the language of the region. Sometimes the broadcast is also available for the whole country in the regional language. There remains still the written religious, philosophical, historiographical, and aesthetic literature. It is, of course, in the interest of the whole of Indonesia, and maybe also of the whole world, that this literature be translated into the national language, so that its rich content can become part of the national heritage of Indonesia. Naturally, part of it will find its way into translations of modern languages, such as English.

*

Thus the conflicts between the rights of ethnic and linguistic minorities to use and preserve their language and the desire of the centralized states to establish the national language have many aspects.

First, how large is the language community of the minority and how important is its culture? In this time of dense transportation and communication we cannot escape the fact that many of the smaller linguistic and cultural groups will disappear into the larger linguistic and cultural group of the nation. It is very often even in the interest of these groups that they merge with larger groups, in order to participate in the progress of the whole nation. For example, if the primary school is in the native language, it is difficult for parents to move to another part of the country with another language. Moreover, the skill in reading and writing is of little advantage if there are no or only a few books in that language available. This does not mean that the linguistic groups cannot use their language in daily life among themselves.

Through the permeation of the minority language with words and thoughts from the larger national language, it is very likely that in a few decades these languages will experience a metamorphosis: they become a kind of dialect of the larger national language.

In this context it is of course most important to know what the aim of the minority group is, in maintaining their language. Very often it has, as has been said, a political aim. The language issue is then only a part of a larger problem of political independence or autonomy.

If it is of a purely cultural character, the central government can take many initiatives to promote the culture or in most cases the arts of that group in the context of the total cultural promotion of the country. Translation and descriptions of the cultural heritage in the national language is of the greatest importance for its preservation and eventual spread.

In concluding this paper, I would like to summarize the present language situation in the world, in order to give an objective picture of the place and the meaning of the minority languages in the total linguistic situation of our time. In the overall social and cultural crisis during the last fifty years, resulting from the density and speed of transportation and communication in the world, the importance and meaning of various languages are going through a rapid transformation.

First there is the rapid spread of modern industrial civilization during the last century and a half which made it the true world civilization of our time, based on the tremendous progress of science and technology and resulting in economic welfare in the advanced countries. Although most countries of the world have not yet reached this scientific, technological, and economic progress of Western Europe, North America, and Japan, many countries are already moving in that direction, while others are still at the beginning of their endeavour to achieve the same aim. In this dominating modern culture with its characteristic scientific, technological, and rational economic thought and concepts, universities, banks, and factories are the main centre of activities and achievements. Viewed from a linguistic standpoint the advanced modern languages, such as French, Japanese, German, and Russian are expressing the same ideas and concepts, which form the core of modern culture or civilization. It will be a great advantage for the cooperation and further development of modern culture as a whole, when the basic notions and concepts of our progressive culture are as far as possible standardized and expressed in the same words, or words deriving from the same root, that they are recognizable in all modern languages. It is to be hoped that UNESCO will be able to take the lead in the coordination of the standardization of the important modern terminologies of the world, for a smooth exchange of ideas and concepts, goods and commodities between the various linguistic areas in the world.

Besides these modern languages which are the bearers of modern cultures, especially after World War II, various national languages have arisen in the newly independent countries of Asia and Africa, such as Hindi in India, Urdu in Pakistan, Singhalese in Sri Lanka, Indonesian in Indonesia, Malaysian in Malaysia, and Tagalog or the Philippine language in the Philippines. In Africa the Swahili language, which has long functioned as the lingua franca in East Africa, has come to the fore. Beside that there are the old languages such as the Mandarin language, which is the official language of one billion Chinese, and the Arab language which is the national and official language from Morocco to the Arab Peninsula, which also have to adjust to modern culture. As we know, Arabic has recently been accepted as one of the official languages of the United Nations.

All these languages are still in the process of becoming modern languages in the rapid process of the modernization of their countries. But most of them are still lacking not only the necessary modern vocabulary of science, technology, and economic progress, but also and especially the whole arsenal of books and reading material which express not only the achievements of our age in science and technology but also the totality of human thought, ideas, and experiences through the centuries. Watching the tremendous speed of progress in science and human knowledge of our time, it is justifiable to ask the question: Will these languages still be able to catch up with the existing advanced modern languages, such as English, French, German,

Russian, and Japanese, through an extensive programme of translation and through the writings of native scholars?

These problems can also be viewed from another standpoint, by asking the question: Is it still worthwhile to achieve this gigantic task, or, to put it differently: Is it not easier and more efficient for these nations to take the existing modern languages as the languages of their modern culture, which is dominated by the progress of science, technology, and economics? An example of the latter is the national language of the Philippines, which derives from Tagalog. Although it is the national language of the Philippines, the medium of instruction in universities and high schools is English. Smaller nations such as Jamaica, Singapore, and various other countries in Africa have already made similar decisions.

But meanwhile there are larger nations such as China, India, Indonesia and others which would like to have their own modern languages. Their problem is how, in the shortest time possible, to modernise their language in order to achieve the level of the advanced modern languages. As I have said before, it is not an easy task: India, for example, is not yet able to discard the English language, apart from the fact that the South Indian states from the very beginning preferred English to Hindi as the national language. Indonesia, which from the very beginning used the Indonesian language as the only official language and the only medium of instruction from primary school to university, is now facing great difficulties in the development of its universities and learning because not enough reading material is available in the Indonesian language, while the command of English, German, etc., is very low among the students and graduates of the universities.

The problem of minority languages, as viewed from this broad perspective, becomes less and less important. We have to accept the fact and the necessity that many of these languages will decrease in importance through compulsory education in the modern national language, and through the increasing density of transportation and communication the world over.

But nevertheless there is, in the whole world, a tendency discernible to come back, not only to the small languages of minorities but also to smaller languages and dialects, because the modern languages, dominated by the rationality and business acumen of modern life, very often have lost their unique characteristics, which are related to the life of the people in the form of folklore, folkbeliefs, folkways and wisdom, with their characteristic art forms, their poetry, and often their countryside romanticism. The Javanese say there is a certain feeling, *rasa*, in the Javanese language which gives them a feeling of satisfaction and life fulfilment which is missing in the official national language with its dry rationality.

For people in young countries who have the task of promoting the modern official national language, there remains nothing but to have a sympathetic heart and eye for these movements and to attempt to absorb, to transmit as much as possible of these folkswisdoms, the unique poetry and other art forms into the modern languages.

Linguistic minorities and language policy in Latin America: The case of Mexico

RODOLFO STAVENHAGEN, *EL COLLEGIO DE MEXICO*

Latin America comprises the countries of the American continent south of the United States, in which the official language is Spanish or Portuguese (Brazil). English or French are spoken in a number of Caribbean island-nations or coastal states, but except for Brazil the concept of Latin America refers mainly to the seventeen independent Spanish-speaking countries. As is well known, Spanish – or, to be exact, Castillian – was introduced by the Spanish conquerors in the sixteenth century and has since become the national language in all of these states.

Less well known is the fact that, despite this process of linguistic homogenization, today there are still over 400 different American Indian ethnic groups in Latin America, each with its own language. The total number of speakers of Indian languages in the region is estimated to be 30 million, that is, about 8.5 % of the Latin American population. Some groups, such as a number of Amazonian tribes, have only a few hundred members each; others may run into the millions, such as the Quechua, Aymara, Maya, and Nahua groups. In most countries, Indian ethnic groups are decidedly national minorities, though they are usually concentrated in certain areas where they constitute a local majority most of the time. But in Bolivia, Peru, Ecuador, and Guatemala they actually constitute numerical majorities.

In Mexico there are over fifty different Indian linguistic groups and altogether they represent approximately 15 % of the national population. They are mainly concentrated in the south and southeast of the country, and in some of the federal states the various Indian ethnic groups represent a majority of the population, particularly in the rural areas. The rest of the national population may be classified as *mestizo*, or culturally and racially mixed. The criteria used for the classification of the country's ethnic groups have varied over the years, but the linguistic criterion has prevailed over others. Still, it may be argued that, from the cultural point of view, Indian ethnic groups are more numerous than would be indicated by the sole use of linguistic considerations. The proportion of Indian monolinguals to bilinguals (Indian language and Spanish) differs from group to group, but in general it may be said that monolingualism has decreased sharply over the last few decades.

The Mexican government has dealt with the linguistic diversity of the population in various ways over the years. In colonial times, the Catholic missionaries used the native languages to convert the population to Christianity. But, on the other hand, Spanish was recognized and used as the language of empire. In the nineteenth century the independent Republic of Mexico abolished all legal distinctions between Indians and non-Indians. All Mexicans were considered equal before the law and Indians were not to be discriminated against, nor to receive any special privileges. Schooling was carried out in Spanish only and the Indian languages were considered a nuisance.

The Mexican social revolution of 1910-1917 put the Indians back again squarely into the limelight. The new social policies were designed to raise the standard of living of the peasants, a large majority of whom were Indians. This was to be achieved through two principal means: land reform and education. Government policy towards the Indian groups was a policy of assimilation and incorporation. The official ideology considered that the Indian communities represented backward social and economic conditions and that development implied their becoming full-fledged members of the national society. In doing so, they would have to abandon their Indian ethnic cultural characteristics, including their native languages, and acquire what is officially called national culture. National culture, of course, is mainly of Spanish origin, though it has incorporated many originally Indian elements over the centuries. And the national culture has a single national language, which is Spanish. Thus, hispanicization of the Indian groups became the mainstay of the Mexican government's policy vis-à-vis the Indian populations.

Educational policy in Mexico is the responsibility of the federal government, and its main instrument is the Ministry of Education. Since the early years after the revolution, the Ministry set up a special Department of Indian Affairs, which has been reorganized on several occasions and is now called Department of Indian Education. There also exists a National Indianist Institute (*Instituto Nacional Indigenista*), whose purpose is to coordinate the various activities of the federal government in the Indian areas.

As late as the 1920s, the Indian population in Mexico was almost totally illiterate. The non-Indian population, particularly in the rural areas, was only slightly more literate. None of the Indian languages had a written standard. To be sure, ancient Maya and Nahuatl had scripts, but these did not survive the Spanish conquest. The grammars and dictionaries of Indian languages prepared by the early missionaries were forgotten. A few select scholars "cultivated" Maya or Nahuatl, using Latin script, but the mother tongues of the Indian groups were all nonwritten languages. Literacy in Spanish was the privilege of only a handful of persons in some of the Indian communities.

In the early 1940s, the government launched a vast adult literacy campaign which managed to reduce illiteracy from over 60 % to less than 30 %, according to official statistics. But it was carried out almost exclusively in Spanish and its impact on the Indian communities was slight. By the 1970s, illiteracy had again become a national problem. It had grown anew over the intervening period because the national school system had not been able to keep up with rapid population growth and because so many rural areas had simply not been covered by the massive educational effort launched by the federal government in the 1920s and 1930s and kept up over the years. Thus, in the mid-1970s another literacy campaign was carried out which by latest counts has been able to reduce illiteracy to around 15 % in 1980. It is difficult to assess the impact of this latest campaign on the Indian groups, because available statistics are not broken down by ethnic group, but it would be safe to guess that again the main progress has probably taken place in the urban and non-Indian areas.

Indianist educational policy has not been concerned so much with adult literacy as with schooling at the primary level. It is here that different objectives, policies, and methods have been applied over the years and that lively debates among scholars and officials have taken place. In the 1920s, the federal government initiated a massive effort to enlarge the educational system by establishing schools in hitherto isolated rural areas. For the first time, backward long-forgotten villages were incorporated into the school network. Hastily trained teachers were sent out into the backwoods, and children in the rural areas were able to learn their three R's. Many monolingual Indian communities received their first contact with the national school system at that time. But the prevailing ideology considered that "being an Indian" was an obstacle to progress and "civilization". School was taught in Spanish, and it was hoped that the Indians would soon learn the "national language", become fully integrated into "national" society, and forget their "backward" customs and manners. The use of the native mother tongue in schools was strictly forbidden. Teachers were sent into the villages from the outside, to transmit the "new" way of life and the "benefits of civilization and culture". Children who spoke their own language in school were considered offenders and punished. They were taught to feel ashamed of their own culture and to despise it. The brighter Indian students were taken out of their communities and sent to boarding schools and special institutions in the cities, where they were expected to become fully "integrated". Many of them, of course, did become so integrated or acculturated to urban ways that they never returned home.

The mediocre results of this policy, and the negligible impact which such schooling had on the community, soon became apparent. By the 1930s a number of voices were raised, demanding a bilingual education and the respect of local cultures and values. A small number of pilot projects in Indian areas were set up, under the supervision of linguists and anthropologists, to test the new ideas about bilingual education and literacy in the native language. The government invited an American-based Protestant missionary organization, the Summer Institute of Linguistics, to come to Mexico and help with this effort. The Institute had some previous experience in developing scripts for nonwritten languages and methods for teaching reading and writing to adults in these languages. Though over the years the Institute did provide technical assistance in these matters and produced a considerable amount of specialized knowledge about Mexico's Indian languages, it was mainly concerned with missionary activity and encountered increasing resistance among many Indian communities and other groups of Mexican society (including teachers and social scientists who accused the Institute of serving foreign political interests). In 1980 the Mexican Government officially severed its relationship with the SIL, but did not expel it or prohibit its private activities, as has happened in many other countries.

During the 1940s and 1950s a small number of devoted linguists and teachers continued working on the unwritten Indian languages, but official interest in these questions waned, and not much progress was achieved.

Indian education, as it were, consisted in the continued expansion of the national rural school system to the Indian areas. Teaching programmes were identical all over the country, regardless of regional or urban-rural cultural differences. All teaching was carried out in Spanish.

Textbooks and programme content were highly biased in favor of middle-class urban outlooks. Those who questioned the wisdom of this approach were answered that it was contrary to a nationalist and democratic viewpoint to establish differential education and that, if some areas or ethnic groups were culturally or economically backward, the national school system would simply have to make an additional effort in order to "raise" the standards of the rural and particularly the Indian population to what was considered to be the national norm.

Among the small groups of specialists who were concerned with Indian education in governmental institutions, serious discussions took place during the 1950s. On the one hand were those who argued that the only way to introduce Spanish as the national vehicular language into the Indian communities was to teach it directly in the same fashion as it was taught in Spanish-speaking environments, and to teach all subjects in Spanish as well. This was the traditional method, and to date many teachers and pedagogues still adhere to it. On the other hand were those who felt that this method could not be successful in an environment where the mother tongue was not Spanish, and they argued for other methods whereby Spanish would be taught as a second language in primary school and even to pre-school children. Several such methods for teaching Spanish as a second language were tried in a number of pilot projects around the country. This meant preparing primers, and training the right kind of personnel. It was felt that the regular subjects of elementary schools could only be taught in Spanish once literacy in this language had been acquired by the Indian schoolchildren.

Still another group of experts maintained the earlier arguments in favour of a bilingual education. They affirmed that literacy, to be successful and meaningful to the children, should be carried out in the native language. Only after the children had mastered the technique of reading and writing in their mother tongue should Spanish be introduced as a subject in itself and be used as the language of teaching all other subjects. The end objective, of course, was still the hispanicization of the Indian school children; literacy in the mother tongue was considered only as a necessary stepping-stone towards this end.

The two basic methods of alphabetization competed with each other for several years (literacy directly in Spanish (with two variants) and literacy first in the mother tongue). Each method had its supporters among specialists as well as in official institutions. The main handicap to the rapid extension of the second method (literacy first in the native language) was the lack of trained teachers competent in each one of the Indian languages and the lack of teaching materials in these languages. Therefore this method, while gradually becoming accepted by officials responsible for Indian education, made only little headway in the 1950s and early 1960s.

Still, efforts were finally being made to train as teachers young men and women from the Indian communities who had at least completed primary schooling themselves or who, in a few exceptional cases, had been to secondary school or teachers college. They had the difficult task, with the help of some linguists, of preparing primers in their own tongues, teaching reading and writing in the mother tongue, teaching Spanish as a second language simultaneously, and, to boot, imparting the basic subjects (natural sciences, arithmetic, history) either in the native language or in Spanish on the basis of the only existing officially provided school textbooks in Spanish.

Obviously, such efforts could not make an impact on the Indian communities unless backed up by massive and sustained support by the federal government. This finally became forthcoming in the middle 1960s. The principle of early literacy in the native language plus the teaching of Spanish as a second language became the official policy, and the training of teachers from the Indian communities became the highest priority of the Indian Education programme.

By the middle of the decade of the seventies, a highly vocal, well-organized group of what became known as "bilingual teachers" from the various Indian ethnic groups had become integrated into the federal school system and was on the federal payroll. Their number increased from a handful in the 1950s to several thousand at the beginning of the 1980s. Most if not all of the over fifty Indian groups now have trained schoolteachers who are able to teach up to at least the third year of elementary school in the Indian language; primers exist in all of the Indian languages, and the official primary school textbooks (produced and distributed by the government at no cost to the students) are gradually being translated into all of these languages and adapted to local cultural contexts. For this purpose, a master's programme for the training of ethnolinguists from the Indian groups was begun in the late 1970s.

Gradually, the "bilingual teachers" have become aware of the wider issues involved in the apparently only technical questions of whether to teach Spanish first or later, or whether literacy should be fostered in the native tongue or in Spanish. For some years now, the bilingual teachers associations, supported by knowledgeable social scientists and public officials, have been demanding not only that the Indian languages be used in the teaching of reading and writing but also have insisted that the whole educational programme in the Indian communities should be truly bilingual and bicultural. This means that, for the first time in the educational history of Mexico, the Indian languages and cultures are being given due recognition in school programmes. It is hoped that all subjects during the whole of the primary school cycle will be taught in the mother tongue, in those areas where this is spoken by a local majority; that Spanish will be introduced from the beginning as a second language and that the Indian students will become fully bilingual; that in all relevant subjects the local culture will be prominently dealt with (for example, local and regional history, geography, customs, traditions, ethnobiology, etc.) At the same time, at the national level, the curriculum should be organised in such a fashion that schoolchildren all over the country will become aware of the pluricultural makeup of their nation, and respect for and knowledge of the minority cultures should become a part of the national curriculum. Of course, the full hispanicization of all minority ethnic groups is still the stated objective, but no longer to the exclusion of the minority cultures as such.

To achieve a truly bicultural educational system, at least in the core areas where the minority ethnic groups are concentrated, will be a long and complicated task, but the first important steps have been taken, and recent governmental decisions lead one to believe that bilingual and bicultural education in the Indian regions are now official policy, in contrast to the earlier policy of assimilation and integration.

China's minorities

JEROLD A. EDMONDSON, *UNIVERSITY OF TEXAS AT ARLINGTON*

Contrary to widespread misapprehension, China is not populated just by the Chinese. Both Taiwan (Republic of China) and the Mainland (People's Republic of China) possess sizable minorities. The PRC recognizes officially fifty-five minority nationalities and seven ethnic groups, aside from the Han majority (see Wang De (1981)). In Taiwan as well, eleven aboriginal Austronesian languages are still spoken.

In this paper I report on the distribution, populations, and genetic affiliation of these groups. Moreover, I sketch the attitude of the ROC and PRC toward these groups generally and toward their languages in particular. Of special interest will be the development of literacy, orthographies, education, and languages research.

The sources of my information include some well-known publications available outside Asia, especially June Teufel Dreyer's *China's Forty Million* (1976), issues of *Minzu Yuwen, China Reconstructs,* and *China Pictorial.* Furthermore, during the summer of 1982 I carried out onsite fieldwork and inspection in Taiwan, Beijing, and Yunnan Province. Two minorities were observed during this period: the Kohkoh Amis in Taiwan (about two months of fieldwork) and the Sani (a Yunnan Yi people, for 2-3 days). Information about linguistic research on minorities has been obtained from Chang Kun (1967) and Li Fang-kuei (1967) and, for the period since 1967, from Wang Jun (1982).

A. The language families

Who then are these minority nationalities and what language families do they belong to? On the Asian Mainland there are, according to Chinese scholars, representatives of the Sino-Tibetan, Altaic, Austro-Asiatic, and Indo-European families within the borders of the PRC. The names of these languages are cited in the romanization adopted by the Third National Convention for Language Planning held in Beijing in January 1980 as reported in Zhu (1980: 78). I do, however, use the Western names *Tibetan* and *Korean* for *Zangzu* and *Chaoxian*[2].

The Sino-Tibetan family has the greatest number of independent languages and also the greatest numbers of speakers, even discounting the Han. Zhang (1980: 122-4) divides the Sino-Tibetan groups into five branches:

(1) *Sino-Tibetan (within China)*

Zhuang Dong branch	Zhuang Dai group — Zhuang, Bouyei, Dai. Dong Sui group — Dong, Sui, Mulam, Maonan. Li group — Li.
Tibeto Burman branch	Tibetan group — Zang (Tibetan), Qiang, Nu, Drung, Primmi, Monba, Lhoba. Yi group — Yi, Lisu, Naxi, Hani, Lahu, Achang, Bai, Tujia, Jino. Jingpo group — Jingpo.
Miao Yao branch	Miao group — Miao Yao group — Yao, Gelo.
Gin language (Vietnamese)	
Han language	all forms of Chinese; also used by Hui, Man(chu), and She nationalities.

Han includes not only the National Language of China, Mandarin Chinese, but also the other manifestations of Chinese, e.g., Cantonese, Hunanese, Wu, Hokkian, etc. Moreover, some minorities have largely adopted Mandarin for everyday communication, e.g., the Hui, Man(chu), and She. Zhuang-Dong, the most populous branch, divides into three groups: Zhuang-Dai, Dong-Sui and Li. The Tibeto-Burman branch also splits into three groups: the Tibetan group, the Yi group (Loloish) with numerous representatives, and the Jingpo group. The Miao-Yao branch is represented by twelve divergent varieties of Miao, the closely related Yao, and one other member.

Geographically, the Sino-Tibetan languages in China are found in the southern half of the country, stretching from the Himalayan highlands, then south of the Yangtze through Sichuan and Yunnan Provinces to the south central provinces of Guizhou and Guangxi. The Li people live on Hainan Island (Guangdong). There are no large tribal homelands in East and Southeast China (the Shezu of Fujian Province may represent a splinter of the Yao nationality who were driven eastward by the Han).

The Altaic languages are also quite numerous and some are large.

(2) *Altaic languages*

Turkish branch — Uygur, Kazak, Salar, Uzbek, Tartar, Kirgiz, Yugur.
Mongol branch — Mongol, Daur, Songxiang, Bonan, Tu.
Tungus branch — Tungus group-Orogen, Ewenki.
　　　　　　　　　　Man(chu) group-Man(chu), Xibe, Hezhen.
Chaoxian (Korean).

Four branches are reported: the Turkish branch, including the languages in Xinjiang Province; the Mongol branch; the Tungus brach with Orogen and Ewenki, the Man(chu) group; and, finally, Korean. These languages straddle China's northern borders with the Soviet Union and Outer Mongolia and are also found around the frontier with North Korea.

The Austro-Asiatic family is represented by a few northern Mon-Khmer languages such as Va, Blang and Benglong. These speakers are found in southern Yunnan Province.

(3) *Austro-Asiatic languages*

Mon-Khmer branch — Wabeng long group Va, Benglong, Blang.

The only Indo-European languages found in China are Russian and Tajik, whose speakers inhabit some areas of Xinjiang Province. Six hundred Russians and 20,000 Tajiks constitute some of the smallest minorities in the entire country.

(4) *Indo-European languages*

Slavic branch — Eastern group — Russian Iranian branch — Tajik.

The Austronesian languages are found among aboriginal peoples in Taiwan. Prof. Tan Hu of the Central Institute for Minorities in Beijing has told me that the work being carried out in the PRC on Austronesian languages is being done by people originally from Taiwan. Nonetheless, Wang De (1981: 10) lists the homeland of the Gaoshan (Formosan Austronesian) as Taiwan and Fujian.

It is interesting to observe that the languages listed here may not represent a complete list of China's minorities. The Jino were only recognized in 1979. Liu (1982) has reported on a group in Sichuan Province that has not as yet been officially recognized, even though this group — the Ersu — has been documented from Tang times. In the future we can expect the list of minorities to grow as their status is clarified.

On the island of Taiwan and a few smaller neighbouring islands eleven aboriginal Austronesian languages are still spoken, see Tsuchida (1976).

(5) *Austronesian languages*

Formosan branch

| Atayalic group — Atayal, Seedeq.
| Tsouic group — Tsou, Rukai.
| Paiwanic group — Saisiyat, Thao, Puyuma,
| Paiwan, Bunun, Amis, Yami.

(From Chen 1982)

B. Size and character of populations

With respect to size, China's minorities on the Mainland and Taiwan range from the 12 million strong Zhuang, who live primarily in Guangxi, to a few hundred Slaves, a few thousand Bonan, Tartar, and Yugur nomads, a few thousand Vietnamese and Primmi Tibetans. Minority nationalities, in total, number 67,233,254, according to the just-completed census, which amounts to 6 % of the entire population (see *People's Daily* of January 27, 1983).

Among other large groups are the Hui Chinese, a group of Moslem Hans descended from a mercenary army sent from Arabia to aid the Tang emperor in 756 A.D. They, unlike many other groups in China, eat no pork; they read Arabic and faithfully practice their religion. Though they share much in common with the Han culturally (aside from religion), intermarriage is not common. Indeed, they do not even live together in their native areas, which are found in Gansu and Qinghai.

The Uygurs before 1949 made up 75 % of the population in Xinjiang Province. They are Turkic and Moslem and yet not totally nomadic. There has been some resistance to Han resettlement in this area. Yet, they have proven less resistant to integration than the more independent-minded and devout Hui. The Uygurs were once a very powerful group in Western China, having occupied much of Mongolia before being driven out to settle in Xinjiang.

The integration of the Hans with the peoples of the South and Southwest is certainly far less advanced. These peoples tend to be fiercely independent, clan-oriented hill tribes, living apart from the Chinese. They have resisted assimilation by the Han for centuries, being presumably the descendents of those mentioned in the *Manshu* (Book of the Southern Barbarians).

Although China's minorities are comparatively unknown abroad, a sizable number of people is involved. Groups having more than one million members are as follows.
(a) Zhuang 12; (b) Hui 6.4; (c) Uygur 5.4; (d) Yi 4.8; (e) Miao 3.9; (f) Tibetan 3.4; (g) Mongol 2.6; (h) Man(chu) 2.6; (i) Bouyei 1.7; (j) Korean 1.6; (k) Yao 1.2; (1) Dong 1.1; and (m) Bai 1. (Figures in millions from Wang De (1981)).

On the island of Taiwan the Amis are the most numerous minority group with 80,000 according to the 1964 census. In fact, some Amis estimate their numbers much higher, at perhaps as much as 300,000. They populate the Eastern coastal plain of the island from Hualian to Taidong. The Amis are known for their colorful singing and dancing, which is especially displayed during an annual harvest festival. The taking of heads was practiced into the period of the Japanese occupation of Taiwan.

The second largest minority group on Taiwan are the Bunun. The 1964 census placed their numbers at 30,000. They inhabit the mountainous area from the central spine of the island to the coastal plain where the Amis live.

Other groups are much smaller in number. The Tsou are said to number less than 4,000, for example.

C. Minority policy of the PRC

The minority policy of the PRC is extraordinarily important to China, certainly far more important than the mere numbers involved. According to Dreyer (1976: 3-4) China has shown special interest in this 6 % of her population because: (a) minorities straddle sensitive borders that traditionally have allowed fluid crossings of humans and material, and loyalty is, presumably, divided between brethren outside China's borders and the Chinese state; (b) minority areas are relatively underpopulated compared to the densely peopled East: (c) minority areas are rich in land and mineral resources and (d) unsatisfied minorities run counter to the aims of a socialist state. That's why the PRC feels it has a "minorities problem". And language is certainly a large part of the problem.

While there have been reversals from time to time, the long-term policy with regard to minority affairs has been one of increasing autonomy. For example, minority areas have been given local self-determination through the establishment of five autonomous regions (AR): Inner Mongolian AR, Xinjiang Uygur AR, Guangxi Zhuang AR, Ningxia Hui AR, and Tibetan AR. . Beyond these autonomous regions, there are also 29 autonomous districts and 67 autonomous counties.

The language policy of the PRC, like the general attitude, has since 1949 been caught on the horns of a dilemma. Should one attempt to assimilate and unify through a common language, Putonghua (the PRC name for Mandarin)? Or try to win the hearts and minds through multilingual opportunity? Should the minority languages be nurtured or should the path of vertical social mobility be paved with knowledge of Mandarin. On the one hand, the binding force of a national language has often been the common bond of diverse states. On the other hand, raising the standard of living and health of minorities can be better served with a literate population. Here again, the tendency has been to grant equal status to minority languages in more and more domains. For instance, the 1954 constitution of the PRC stated that citizens of all nationalities had the right to use their own spoken and written languages in court proceedings and had the right to have interpreters. Article 4 of the 1975 constitution, however, guarantees the right quite generally. All nationalities have the freedom to use their own spoken and written languages.

During the Cultural Revolution, minority policy, like many other policies, was fundamentally disrupted. Since 1976, there has been a wholesale re-establishment of minorities' institutions and a flurry of publications of past and present work. Recently, China's minorities have enjoyed more exposure to an international public. This change has been increasingly evident from the year 1980 onward. For example, *The National Geographic* published its map of The Peoples of China in the July 1980 issue. In 1981 the minority dance troup of the Central Institute went on tour of the US. And, in 1982, the 15th International Conference on Sino-Tibetan Languages and Linguistics was held in Beijing. Minority languages was one of the major programme items of this conference.

D. *Minority policy of the ROC*

The situation of minorities on Taiwan is quite different from that on the Mainland. Only Guoyu (the ROC name for Mandarin) is an official language, and all education and government contact is conducted in it. Minority languages as well as other forms of Chinese enjoy only unofficial use. Minorities have no special language status, because the aboriginals constitute only 1.6 % of the population and, thus, make up only one of the smaller groups of people not natively speaking Mandarin. Moreover, they have no tribal relatives outside of Taiwan. They generally live in less desirable mountainous areas and do not count as a destabilizing influence. Nevertheless, the state has been concerned about the lower standard of living enjoyed by these minorities and has provided compensation in terms of tax incentives. All the minority people I interviewed were quite satisfied with the current government and compared it favorably with the Japanese occupation, though, ironically, many of the older generation spoke Japanese better than Mandarin.

Because of the lack of official support, the language situation in aboriginal areas is in flux. In the village of Kalalaq near Juisui, I found that older people normally used Amis (with code switching into Japanese) in everyday communication. People under the age of twenty preferred Mandarin. This schizo-phrenia revealed itself in dramatic fashion during the mass I attended in the village church. The French missionary priest conducted services bilingually in Amis, for the older generation, and in Mandarin, for the younger. Without the support of written language and governmental interest, the prognosis for Taiwan's remaining aboriginal languages is not good.

E. *Linguistic research on minority languages*

Before 1950, the Chinese were themselves uncertain what ethnic and language groups dwelled within their borders. Nevertheless, some important work was carried out by foreign and Chinese scholars on some of the larger groups: the Mongols, the Tibetans, the Man(chu), and the Uygur. Wang Jun (1982: 2) cites pre-war work by Zhao Yuanren (Chao Yuen-ren), Wang Qingru, Yu Daoquan, Li Fanggui (Li Fang-kuei), and Fu Maoji. During the Second World War some of the scholars active in China were the following: Ma Xueliang, Fu Maoji, Xing Gongwan, Zhang Kun (Chang Kun), and Li Fanggui.

After 1949 the basic guidelines for dealing with language research on minorities were: (a) to concentrate on practical matters, (b) to help the minorities to develop and reform their writing systems, (c) to cooperate with local research projects, (d) to help raise the level of the minority cadre, (e) to note the use and sociolinguistic situation as well as carry out descriptive linguistic research.

In order to carry out this policy, the Linguistic Research Institute of the Chinese Academy of Sciences (reestablished 1977 as National Minorities Studies Institute under the Chinese Academy of Social Sciences, see Fingar 1981: 226), was founded in June 1950. In 1951, a sister institution, the Central Institute for Minorities, was founded in Beijing under the Ministry of Education.[2] Its mission was to educate professionals among minorities in history, spoken language, art, and literature of non-Han peoples. Moreover, many of the provinces with large minority populations established their own Minority Institutes. Today, the following institutions are devoted to research on and education of minority people: Inner Mongolia University (Hohhot, Inner Mongolia Autonomous Region), Xinjiang University (Urumqi, Xinjiang Autonomous Region), Northwest Institute for Nationalities (Lanzhou, Gansu Province), Southwest Institute for Nationalities (Chengdu, Sichuan Province), Yunnan Institute for Nationalities (Kunming, Yunnan Province), Qinghai Institute for Nationalities (Xining, Qinghai Province), Tibet Institute for Nationalities (Xianyang, Shaanxi Province), Guangxi Institute for Nationalities (Nanning, Guangxi Autonomous Region), Guangdong Institute for Nationalities (Baoting County, Guangdong Province) and Yanbian University (Yanji County, Jilin Province).

Once the research institutes and linguistic teams had been established, the next order of business was to conduct surveys of minority nationality areas. Most of this work was accomplished in the 1950s by teams sent out from the National Minorities Institute. The ten-year period of turbulence that followed largely stopped research in this area as generally in the country.

With respect to the publication of research results, the quarterly journal *Minzu yuwen* (Nationality languages) has, over the years, become the most frequent organ for publication of article-length contributions. Beyond the periodicals, there is a regularly appearing series of "Introductions" and "Outlines" of the grammars of minority languages. The second of these are usually book-length treatments in some detail, while the "Introductions" are shorter. Todate more than thirty have appeared, including: Tibetan, Yi, Bai, Qiang, Hani, Naxi, Jingpo, Drung, Lhoba, Zhuang, Dong, Sui, Li, Miao, Yao, Uygur, Salar, Mongol, Tu, Daur, Dongxiang, Xibe, Orogen, Tajik, Va, Primmi, Jino, and Bonan. Among the "Outlines" are sketches of Zhuang, Bouyei, Dai, Dong, and Mongol. There is also a tradition of dictionary-making for national languages that began after 1949 with a 26,000-entry volume on Tibetan. In the watershed year 1980 no fewer than five bilingual dictionaries appeared.

In addition to the more practical projects of orthographic reforms, grammatical outlines and dictionaries, there has also been considerable research on questions of the individual sound systems of these languages and comparisons for historical reconstruction and determination of genetic relationships. This work promises to be especially useful in fleshing out our picture of the Sino-Tibetan language family.

Another area of interest in the PRC is the study of tones and classifiers in these languages, since these traits are among the most characteristic areal features of East Asian languages. Special aspects of phonology have also received considerable interest, e.g., consonant clusters, tense/lax vowel contrasts, as well as vowel harmony in the Turkish group. A recent bibliography of research in the PRC on minority languages can be found in Fu (1982).

While the Central Institute emphasizes education and research at the national level, the provincial institutes do the same at the local level. Their mission is to improve technical knowledge among minorities. For example, the Yunnan Institute of Minorities, Kunming, was converted after the Cultural Revolution from training minorities as cadre members of the Communist Party into an institution of higher learning. At present it has 1500 students and 7 departments: Language and Literature, Economics and Management, History, Mathematics, Physics, and Foreign Language. 97 % of all students are ethnic minorities. The language of instruction is Mandarin. There is also a kind of intensive prepsection for students with weak backgrounds. Students are enrolled at the time of the National Entrance Examination every year.

The Yunnan Institute of Minorities, like the Central Institute in Beijing, is also charged with language development and research. In Kinming at present four indigeneous languages are being taught: two Dai languages as well as Lisu and Jingpo. Soon, a section will be opened to research the Va, Lahu, and Yi languages.

In the ROC for the last few years most of the research on minority languages has been carried out at the highest academic institution, the Academia Sinica, in the outskirts of Taipei. At this institute one linguist, Paul Jenkuei Li, works full time on Austronesian languages. There have also been small projects in the past. This work is of high quality and employs the methods of modern linguistic field work and analysis. Much of it has appeared in English in the *Bulletin* and *Special Publications of the Institute of History and Philology, Academia Sinica.* In these series, major work after 1967 (see Li Fang-kuei 1967 for earlier items) includes studies on Rukai and Thao phonology, aspects of Tsou, and comparative morphology of Formosan languages by Li Jen-kuei, a monograph on Bunun topic and focus by Jeng Heng-hsiung.

In addition to the work on Austronesian, the *Bulletin* and *Special Publications of the Academia Sinica* have contained work on minority languages of the Mainland. Notable are the contributions of Li Fang-kuei on Dai languages as well as those of Betty Shefts Chang and Chang Kun on Tibetan, Gyarong, and other Sino-Tibetan languages.

F. Orthographies

Some of China's larger groups have traditional writing systems that are not of modern invention. In this group there are those with a rich liturgical and secular literature such as Tibetan, Uygur, Mongol, and Man(chu). There are also those script systems borrowed from neighbouring languages outside China that are of more recent date. In this second subgroup are Yi, which uses a Lao/Thai-based orthography, and Dai, which uses two systems: the Dehong Dai use a Lao/Thai-based orthography, whereas the Xishuangbanna (a minorities area at the southern tip of Yunnan) Dai use a syllabary based on the southern Burmese. Beyond these two, the Naxi have developed their own traditional system of pictograph writing, known as *dongbazi* or *dongbajing* (see He (1982)).

The Mongol, Uygur, and Man(chu) share a common heritage in regard to writing. According to Jagchid and Hyer (1979: 210-5), the Uygur script, which itself may have come from Aramaic or Sogdian via the Nestorian Christians, has been used by all of them. Mongol records indicate that the Uygur scholar Tatatunggha was captured by Genghis Khan in 1204 and, because of his intelligence, put in charge of the royal seals and writing down of Mongolian in Uygur script. In 1600 the Man(chu) also adopted the signs of the Uygur people, though few ever learned to read it.

In China Uygur script with modifications is still in use today. This is not to say that changes haven't been tried. Under Soviet influence, Outer Mongolia adopted Cyrillic writing officially in 1946. This development was also advocated during the period of Soviet cooperation with China after 1949 but waned with the departure of the Russians.

The Tibetan syllabary traces its origins to the northern Gupta alphabet of India. It was adopted for Tibetan in the 7th century and is still in use today.

The situation in Yunnan Province is especially complex. Of 24 non-Han languages only eight had writing systems before 1949. As already mentioned, Tibetan, Yi, Naxi, and Dai had traditional systems and Lahu, Lisu, Va, and Jingpo had been provided with Latin-based systems by Western missionaries. There are many problems with these orthographies. Often the writing system for one group was borrowed by a neighbouring, perhaps genetically unrelated language. Nearly always the Procrustean bed of a Dai syllabary, for instance, was totally unsuited for a Mon-Khmer language such as Blang or Benglong with complex consonant clusters. Moreover, some writing systems employed *ad hoc* devices that proved to be cumbersome. For instance, James O. Fraser used all capitals with some signs inverted in writing Lisu, e.g., Li SU ꓕO ꓕFO, SO DU (*Lisu Reader*). While setting such signs in type or hand printing is quite easy with this system, typewriting or telegraphy is quite impossible. Nonetheless, retooling is hard and some Lisu groups in China continue to use this old system.

Since 1950 new systems have been developed for Naxi, Bai, Yi, Miao, and Lahu. Others have been improved. Lisu and Lahu, for example, employ no diacritics to indicate the six tones; these are marked by means of final consonants, e.g., in Lahu tone $1 = -\phi$, $2 = -1$, $3 = -d$, $4 = -q$, $5 = -r$ and $6 = -t$ and Lisu employs nearly identical conventions. Instead of inverted letters modern Lisu uses double graphs to indicate the third voice contrast, e.g. b, p, bb and d, t, dd, etc.; for example *bbiat* 'bec', *ol bel* 'two combs'.

In other provinces new systems have been developed. The language of Guizhou, Bouyei, for example, began its written tradition in 1956. It uses 28 Latin-based characters and 5 special tone symbols. The graphs, j, q, w, and, z are not used and the usual Latin alphabet has been enriched with $<$q, a, ɯ, ə, o, η$>$. $<$q, a$>$ are needed to signify special tensed labial and alveolar sounds.

In order to spread literacy in the new or reformed orthographies, the Yunnan National Minorities Press has published a series of books called *Sweep away illiteracy* in most of the 24 languages. There are also collections of stories and advice about health and economic improvement.

In Taiwan I have familiarity with only the writing system of Amis. It (like the others, I am told) employs Latin characters. Only four vowels and sixteen consonant symbols are needed, inasmuch as voiced stops are not found. The problem with the system as it now stands lies in its redundancy. Instead of marking only distinctive contrasts a kind of *ad hoc* phonetic writing has been used. This confuses the reader, since a native speaker already knows where to change the phonetic value of a given segment. While the improvements needed here are not large in number, they are important for improving learnability.

G. Conclusion

Therefore, the language situation for non-Han minorities is at present as fovourable as it ever has been in the PRC. The Central and Provincial Institutes are beginning to open to foreign scholars. This must certainly be viewed as a sign that China feels confident about the course of development of these aspects of domestic policy. Scholars in the area may now be able to study these important links to other SE Asian and Central Asian languages, if not on site, at least in Institutes. First exchanges should take place within a year.

In Taiwan there is no problem to get access to minorities (in some places special police permission is required to enter an area). It is only that the tendency toward assimilation is strong, perhaps inevitable, and the need is to document these most archaic of Austronesian languages before they disappear.

Notes

1 I have written the language name without −*zu* 'group, tribe' when referring to the name of the language and kept the form with − *zu* for the name of the people.
2 In the names of organizations dealing with minorities I have used "minorities" interchangeably with "nationalities". The latter is perhaps a better translation, but English-speaking Chinese regularly employ "minorities". Thus, "Central Institute for Minorities" is equal to "Central Institute for Nationalities".

Bibliography

Chen, Teresa. 1982. *Verbal constructions and verbal classification in Nataoran-Amis.* University of Hawaii Dissertation.

Chang Kun. 1969. National languages. In T. Sebeok (ed.) *Current trends in linguistics. Vol II. Linguistics in East Asia and South East Asia.* The Hague and Paris: Mouton.

Dreyer, June Teufel. 1976. *China's Forty Million: minority nationalities and national integration in the People's Republic of China.* Cambridge, MA: Harvard University Press.

Fingar, Thomas. 1981. *Higher Education and research in the People's Republic of China: Institutional profiles.* Washington: Committee on Scholarly Communication with the PRC, National Academy of Science and National Assoc. for Foreign Student Affairs.

Fu Maoji (ed.). 1982. *Minzu yuwen yanjiu wenji.* (Collection of research articles on national languages). Xining: Qinghai minzu chubanshe (Xining: Qinghai Nationalities Publishing Society).

Grosvenor, Grover. 1980. The people of China (map). *National Geographic.* Washington: National Geographic Society.

He Zhiwu. 1982. *Naxizu dongbajing yuyan shixi.* (Analysis of the linguistics of Naxi pictograph writing). Yunnansheng Lishi Yanjiusuo (Yunnan Provincial Institute of Historical Research). Manuscript.

Jagchid, Sechin and Paul Hyer. 1979. *Mongolia's culture and society.* Boulder, CO: Westview Press/Folkstone: Dawson.

Li Fang-kuei (Li Fanggui). 1967. Linguistics in Taiwan. In T. Sebeok (ed.) *Current trends in linguistics, Vol II. Linguistics in East Asia and South East Asia.* The Hague and Paris: Mouton.

Liu Huigiang. 1982. *Ersuyu gaiyao.* (Outline of the Ersu language). Sichuansheng Minzu Yanjiusuo (Sichuan Provincial Nationalities Research Institute). Manuscript.

Tsuchida, Shigeru. 1976. *Reconstruction of Proto-Tsouic phonology.* Study of Languages and Cultures of Asia and Africa, Monograph Series No. 5. Tokyo: Tokyo Gaikokugo Daigaku.

Wang De. 1981. *Zhongguo de shaoshu minzu.* (China's minorities). Zhongguo (China pictorial) 1.8-13.

Wang Jun. 1982. Zhongguo shaoshu minzu yuyan yanjiu gingkuang. (The situation of research on the linguistics of Chinese minority languages). In Fu (Ed.). *Minzu yuwen yanjiu wenji.* Collection of research articles on national languages). Xining: Qinghai minzu chubanshe (Xining: Qinghai Nationalities Publishing Society).

Zhang Gongjing. 1980. *Guanyu woguo minzu mincheng han yuyan mincheng waiwen yimin de tongyi wenti.* (On standardizing foreign-language transcriptions of China's nationality names and language-family names). Yuwen xiandaihua 3.114-24.

Zhang Kun. 1967. same as Chang Kun. 1967.

Zhu Gong. 1980. Wonguo minzu mincheng de pinfa. (Spelling of China's nationalities' names) *Minzu yuwen* 1.77-8.

The concept of language standardisation and its application to the Indonesian language

S. TAKDIR ALISJAHBANA, *UNIVERSITAS NASIONAL, JAKARTA*

1. Standardization as a problem of social behaviour

In its very essence the problem of standardization is the problem of social behaviour through which the individual communicates with his fellow members in the social group, because it is in the interaction within the social group that the members of the group need a basic uniformity of behaviour and concept, so that there is understanding and communication among them. Only through common forms of behaviour based on common concepts is it possible to arrive at a certain social integration, i.e., that the social group becomes efficiently organized to achieve its goals, its system of values. In this connection all social behaviour in an integrated social group is standardized behaviour. Through this standardized behaviour the members of the group can act and behave with confidence and efficiency within the social group. Everyone knows the meaning of the behaviour of his fellow members and also knows how his fellow members will react or respond to his behaviour. In this sense standardized behaviour within a certain integrated group is the generally expected behaviour.

In every society the generally expected behaviour is determined by social norms. In a face-to-face relationship within a primary group or *Gemeinschaft* the norms take the form of mores and folkways. In a modern social group, which is also called secondary group or *Gesellschaft*, above the mores and folkways develop the more abstract and consciously created laws and other regulations. It is through these mores, folkways, and laws, with the threat of their sanctions, that the social group determines the behaviour of its members, and thus achieves its values.

Viewed from the standpoint of social behaviour in the broadest sense, every language as part of the totality of social behaviour of an integrated social group is standardized, because it is only through a certain uniformity in the use of words and language rules that the members of the social group can understand and communicate with each other efficiently. In this sense the rules of the grammar of any language are only part and parcel of the norms and especially of the mores and folkways of society.

2. The standardization of modern languages

While the standardized character of the small tribe or clan language in a small social group within a limited area is an obvious fact, owing to the dense interaction and communication between the speakers, the rise of the great national languages in Europe and later in the Asian countries, stretching out over extended areas and inhabited by people speaking different dialects and sometimes even languages, brought about problems of conscious and purposeful standardization. For the large European languages such as English, German, French, Italian, etc., which were established during the centuries after the Renaissance parallel to the creation of larger social units of nations, we know that besides political and administrative factors, progress in the means of transportation and communication, especially in the invention of the printing press and the translation of the Bible, has played an important role towards the unification and standardization of these languages.

The problem of standardization in a stricter sense, like the creation of a standard of correct language usage, became especially acute in Europe in the eighteenth century. According to Albert C. Baugh it was an age one of whose first characteristics was "a strong sense of order and the value of regulation. Adventurous individualism and the spirit of independence characteristic of the previous era give way to a desire for system and regularity. This involves conformity to a standard that the consensus of opinion recognizes as good."[1] It was this intellectual tendency which is "seen quite clearly in the eighteenth century efforts to standardize, refine and fix the English language. In the period under consideration discussion of the language takes a new turn. Previously interest had been shown chiefly in such questions as whether English was worthy to be used for writings in which Latin had long been traditional, whether the large additions being made to the vocabulary were justified, and whether a more adequate spelling could be introduced. Now for the first time attention was turned to the grammar, and it was discovered that English had no grammar."[2] In the regularization of the language through grammar, the second half of the eighteenth century showed great progress. "Whereas fewer than fifty writings on grammar, rhetorics, criticism, and linguistic theory have been listed for the first half of the eighteenth century, and still fewer for all the period before 1600, the publication in the period 1750-1800 exceeded two hundred titles. And most of these were concerned in whole or in part with solecisms, barbarisms, improprieties, and questions of precision in the use of English."[3]

The establishment of compulsory education in the European countries in the last century has finally stabilized the position of the standard languages until our age.

 3. Problems of language standardization of the young Asian nations

Parallel problems were faced when the Asian countries within the last century awoke through their contact with European societies and cultures. The Asian people, the colonized as well as the independent ones, gradually realized that their defeat or weakness vis-à-vis the Europeans was caused by the weaknesses and inadequacies in their own societies and cultures. They had to change many of their basic attitudes, concepts, and ways of life, if they wanted to participate in the scientific, economic, and technological progress of the modern world. This consciousness increased even more when many of their children attended English, French, Dutch schools, etc., in Asia as well as in Europe. We all know that as a result of this education national movements started in the various countries of Asia, aiming at the liberation from their colonial masters, and their participation in the progress of the modern world. These facts suddenly dynamized the Asian societies and cultures. Viewed from the standpoint of their integration, these societies and cultures lost their tranquility and uniformity. Many of the actions and institutions which in traditional society were considered true, good, beautiful, even holy, lost their value in the light of the new ideals and ways of thinking. A new generation which through its modern education has arrived at a new system of values, and a new way of life comes to the fore. The changes which in Europe had taken place gradually since the Middle Ages from an expressive culture, i.e., a culture orientated towards religious and aesthetic values based on feeling, intuition, and imagination, into a progressive modern culture dominated by science, economics, and technology, are taking place in Asia in a relatively short period of time. The whole society and culture is in rapid change, even in revolution.

4. The Indonesian linguistics situation

I have tried to describe this situation in the Indonesia of the last century in my collection of essays *Indonesia: Social and Cultural Revolution.*[4] In the great process of *Umwertung aller Werte* the language problems as part and especially as the medium of the social and cultural revolution take more gigantic proportions.

There is first of all the Indonesian linguistic situation, resulting from the character of the country as an archipelago covering one-seventh of the equator, consisting of thousands of islands, of which the largest are further subdivided into many small isolated parts. Over the centuries no less than two hundred and fifty languages and dialects have come into being, although most of them belong to the Malay or Indonesian language group, which is again a part of the larger Malay-Polynesian or Austronesian language group. In the intercourse and communication between the various groups speaking various languages in the Indonesian archipelago, a certain *lingua franca* gradually came into being which has its source in the Malay language, the language of the most restless wandering people in South-East Asia. As the *lingua franca* in such an extended area, it was not possible for the Malay language to be a standardized language. It was a language which through its simple structure quickly adjusted itself not only to the situation in the harbour and the market place, but which has easily tolerated a mixture with local languages and dialects, as well as with foreign languages.

In the haphazard and superficial encounters in commerce, politics, etc., between people speaking different languages, there was no need for a language with a clear standard of correct usage. This need became manifest only much later, at the time when the Dutch colonial government, through the expansion of the colonial administration, considered it necessary to build schools for Indonesians, in order to acquire some trained local civil servants and clerks for government and private enterprises. In order to function as the medium of instruction in schools, the Malay language needed to be standardized. It was the great achievement of C. A. van Ophuysen that he was able to standardize the spelling, the word structure, as well as the syntax of the Malay language which, under the name of "school" or "high" Malay, dominated the language of schools and the administration during four decades of this century.

This standardized "school" or "high" Malay of the early decades of this century, however, although important as a forerunner of the Indonesian language, was still very limited. It was the medium of instruction in primary schools, in training colleges for teachers for schools outside Java, and in the Malay area around Jakarta. In some primary and secondary schools in Java, Malay was also taught as a subject. Although it could be considered the second official language in the Dutch Indies, its influence in Indonesian society at large, and especially in circles of the Indonesian elite, was negligible. The language used by the press and in meetings of political and other institutions was still of the character of the unstandardized Malay *lingua franca,* with great variations in vocabulary and rules of grammar. The real official language and that of modern culture of that time was undoubtedly the Dutch language. For large groups of Indonesians it opened the door not only to leading and better paid positions in the colonial hierarchy, but it also offered the possibility of further study and the means to participate in the progress of science, economics, technology of the modern world. Small wonder that it was especially this education in the Dutch language which was the aspiration of the Indonesian middle class, so that very soon it became clear that the Dutch government was not able to provide for the growing need of Indonesians for Dutch education. Meanwhile a large Dutch group in the colonial society realized that Dutch modern education, instead of bringing more stable and peaceful relations in the colony, on the contrary threatened to create increasing dissatisfaction among educated Indonesians, who began to claim more and more political and economic rights. Moreover, this group started to defend its privileged political and economic position in the colony.

5. The birth of the Indonesian language and its early development.

The limited availability of Dutch education for Indonesians, at the end of the 1920s, led many Indonesians to realize gradually that education through the Dutch language would never reach the great mass of their people. The growing conviction that only through the unity of the Indonesian people would it be possible to build up a force strong enough to face the colonial power, forced the Indonesians to look for another language which could unite all the people of Indonesia. It was this conviction which resulted in the well-known oath of the Indonesian youth of October 28, 1928, of *one country, one nation* and *one language,* all called Indonesian.

For the political aim of uniting the Indonesian people, the Indonesian language undoubtedly proved to be a good solution, but it was clear from the outset that as the language of education from primary school to university, and especially as the language of science, economics, and technology it would not match and replace the Dutch language. Although some improvement had been made during the 1930s in the language, especially as the language of modern literature and social communication, it was not earlier than during the Japanese occupation that Indonesian was confronted with its task as the language of school, administration, and modern communication. It was at that time that language standardization became a pressing problem, which to a certain extent was only part of the process of modernization.

The need to standardize the language became first apparent in the schools, when Dutch was suddenly forbidden. Indonesian suddenly had to fulfill the role of a full-fledged modern language as the medium of instruction from primary school to university. A committee came into being which had the task of translating in the shortest possible time all Dutch textbooks for junior and senior high schools. It was especially in translating various textbooks that the need was felt for a systematic coining and standardization of new terms, so that within a short time the translators, later helped by a team of experts and other interested people, decided to come together regularly to discuss and to coordinate the terms of the various school subjects. Soon, however, in the other fields such as administration, law, medicine, mining, agriculture, etc. the need was also felt for a systematic coining and standardization of terms. As it was also in the interests of the Japanese administration to improve the Indonesian language, it could not but establish a large committee for dealing with modernization and standardization of the Indonesian language. This committee was the *Komisi Bahasa Indonesia*, which was established in 1942. Its task was to improve the language for its broadening function after the elimination of the Dutch language.

To lend this committee high prestige, its membership included not only the most prominent Indonesian writers, linguists, and cultural leaders, but also political celebrities, such as Sukarno and Hatta. Hatta himself was for many years personally active as chairman of the section in charge of scientific and technical terminology. I functioned as Expert Secretary of the committee and at the same time as Head of the Language Office, which prepared and acted upon the committee's decisions.

The committee was, from the beginning, divided into three sections with the respective tasks of:

1. determining a new technical and scientific terminology,
2. writing a new grammar, and
3. selecting words of daily usage.

The section for determining technical and scientific terminology was of course the most important and urgent one. Its task was concrete and limited in scope. Several persons already engaged in translating Dutch textbooks were able to provide the committee with lists of Dutch terms and some tentative Indonesian equivalents. To complete these lists the committee asked teachers who taught various subjects in schools to submit lists of terms used during the initial months after schools had been reopened. In this way the committee had at its disposal several lists or terms of, e.g., botany as they were provisionally used in schools. The task of the staff of the secretary at the language office was to compare the various Indonesian terms, to subject them to severe criticism, and to try to collect other relevant information from additional sources. As a rule the staff then made a choice among various terms in the lists, occasionally introducing new words which were considered more appropriate. The new list of terms arrived at through this process was sent to the botany teachers in Jakarta. About a week thereafter the committee invited them to a meeting for a preliminary decision on these terms, with other people who by profession or for other reasons were considered competent in botany. The group attending this first session was called the subsection of botany, consisting of persons with the same subject of study or interest. The decision of this meeting was mimeographed and sent to the members of the section on terminology for a second decision at a higher level. The section on terminology had to decide on all technical and scientific terms, and consisted therefore of members from different fields and professions. The words decided upon in a given subsection were studied and coordinated with the terms decided upon in other subsections, e.g., in that of zoology, etc. After a certain number of lists dealing with different subjects had been decided upon in this section, the secretary would arrange a plenary meeting of the committee, where the terms were formally confirmed. The first set of terms arrived at in this way was published by the Japanese military authorities in the official Government Gazette and thus received the official sanction of the Japanese government.

The selection and determination of words of daily usage was important, since so many words from dialects and, regional or foreign languages penetrated into the Indonesian language. As pointed out above, already as *lingua franca* the Indonesian language had adjusted itself to local, regional and foreign languages throughout Indonesia. Thus the question is relevant which words could be considered to belong to the generally accepted Indonesian language, and which words should still be considered as foreign, regional, or dialectal elements. The committee in charge of the selection and determination of words in daily usage looked through the vocabulary of newspapers and other mass media, of books, etc. There are of course many words which were accepted as Indonesian words without discussion. In the period of transition all "high" or "school' Malay words of the list of Van Ophuysen were accepted as the core of the Indonesian vocabulary, although later some of them fell into disuse. Many words, however, still bear the mark of the Jakarta dialect, the Javanese, Minangkabau, Dutch, English language, etc. If such a word was encountered, the committee could decide that it already belonged to the accepted Indonesian vocabulary. This committee was especially necessary, since Van Ophuysen's list of school Malay was very limited, consisting of not more than 10,130 words, and some teachers at that time rejected words which were not on the list. It is clear that in the fast-expanding vocabulary of daily usage through the tremendous expansion of Indonesian, this committee was not very useful, since it could not keep pace with the speed of the growth of the language. What was really needed was a descriptive dictionary, registering and explaining the most common words. It is also clear that such a dictionary must be revised regularly and often. In the further development of the planning of the Indonesian language this Committee was not continued.

6. A reformulation of the concept of standardization

The attempts to determine modern Indonesian terminology and the selection and determination of acceptable Indonesian words are clear efforts to standardize the Indonesian language. Standardization in this sense, however, is only a determination of uniform usage. But in the context of language planning — or, as I prefer to say, language engineering — it is necessary at this point to discern at least two levels of standardization.

English spelling, for example, is a standardized spelling, since we can say without exaggeration that every educated Englishman pronounces and writes the English words in the same way. But if we compare, for example, how the various phonemes are written in English, we discover that the spelling is not standardized, because the phoneme /ə/ is writen in English as: *a* in *a*lone, *ai* in moun*ta*in, *e* in system, *eo* in dunge*o*n, *i* in eas*i*ly, *ia* in parl*ia*ment, *o* in gall*o*p, *oi* in porp*oi*se, *ou* in curi*ou*s, *u* in circ*u*s. Viewed from this point there is also no standardization in the relation between the pronunciation and writing of the English words: *I* and *eye, son* and *sun* are pronounced in the same way, although the written images are quite different. It is a known fact, that there are very few rules for the writing of English words, that there exists no relation between the English pronunciation and its written form. In this sense we can say that the English language does not take advantage of the simplicity and efficiency of the Latin alphabet, with its twenty-six letters, for representing its phonemic system. Written English words are nearly comparable to the Chinese script: one must know how a word is written as a whole. An analysis of phonemes and letters will not be of much help. For its 40 phonemes it has about 2000 symbols. English educationalists have long complained about the burden English children have to bear in learning to read.

They have estimated that, because there is no intimate relationship between pronunciation and spelling, the English child needs up to two years more than children of other nations with more regular spelling systems to command the simple art of reading.[5]

7. Indonesian word and syllable structure

In the standardization of their languages the young countries of Asia have to aspire to a higher level of standardization, so that their languages will be much simpler and easier to learn than English. The English words, for example, do not have a characteristic structure or pattern, and foreign words which have been accepted during the centuries more or less retain their original phonemic structure or spelling. With regard to the Indonesian language, it is still possible to determine its word structure on the basis of the simple Malay word pattern. As an agglutinative language its words show a very simple structure, which changes only by adding a limited number of simple syllables or morphemes. According to the hypotheses of Brandstetter[6] and Dempwolff[7] on the structure of the syllables of Ur- or prime-Indonesian, the Indonesian words were originally monosyllabic like Chinese. The mono-syllabic words developed, according to their theory, into polysyllabic ones through the addition of affixes by multiplication and composition.

In counting the syllables of the present Indonesian words in the diction-aries of S. M. Zain and Poerwadarminta, a study by Mr. Sudarno revealed that the great majority of Indonesian words consists of two or three syllables (75 % and 18 %). Monosyllabic words are an exception and very often related to onomatopoeia and interjections, while four syllable words are derived through affixation or compounding. Another possibility is that they are loan words, for example, from Sanskrit.

The further development of the Indonesian vocabulary should retain this simple structure as far as possible in the creation of new words or in the assimilation of words from the dialects and from regional or foreign languages.

It seems that Van Ophuysen, in his *Kitab Arti Logat Melayu*, already realized at the turn of the century, the simplicity and regularity of the Indo-nesian word pattern, because in his word list, with a few exceptions, only two-and three-syllable words are included.

The structure of Indonesian syllables is even simpler. There are only four possibilities:

V	in *a*-kan, su-*a*-ra, ba-*u*
CV	in *ka-mi, me-ja, sa-ya.*
VC	in *is*-lam, mu-*ak*

CVC in *han-tam, hen-dak, pan-tang*

In sharp contrast to Indo-European languages, such as, Dutch, English and German, Indonesian syllables have no consonant clusters. These four syllabic forms are further limited by the fact that mute e /ə/ cannot be used in open or closed end-syllables.

The acceptance of so many words from the dialects and regional languages through the rapid spread of the Indonesian language throughout Indonesia, and the acceptance of so many words from modern languages through contact with modern culture, has during the last decades threatened to destroy the easy and simple Indonesian word and syllable structure. An avalanche of consonant clusters has been introduced by these new loan words. From the Javanese language, words such as *klana, kliru, prabot, trap, trampil, swara, kopyor* are accepted in Indonesian. From Dutch and English: *blouse, crediet/credit, glas/glass, klas/class, proces/process, spiraal/spiral, stop*, etc.

Since the syllable structure of Indonesian words is related to phonetic changes in words with the prefix *me-*, consonant clusters at the beginning of words pose some problems, as is testified by the following examples: The prefix *me-* changes the phoneme *k* of the word *kirim, kejar* into a kind of nasalization *mengirim, mengejar*. The word *kritik*, deriving from the Dutch *kritiek* or the English *critique*, when acquiring the prefix *me-*, becomes *mengritik/mengkritik*. If the word, however, becomes first adjusted to the Indonesian word structure: *keritik*, the prefixation will follow regularly the Indonesian affixation pattern: *mengeritik*. Analogous to this, the English word *stop*, adjusted to the Indonesian word structure, becomes *se-top*. The nasalization with the prefix *me-* should then be *menyetop*, analogous to *sebut*, which becomes *menyebut*. Since there are no mute *e's* in the final syllables of Indonesian words, Javanese words such as *catet, sedep, mantep*, become *catat, sedap, mantap* in Indonesian. The same goes for the Dutch words *kamer, schoener*, which in Indonesian become *kamar, sekonar*. The mute *e* in open syllables also becomes *a* in Indonesian. Thus the Dutch words *acte, analyse* become *akta, analisa*, or *analisis*. If this structure is maintained in the new loan words, the Indonesian language will be able to maintain its simple word and syllable structure throughout its total vocabulary. On the basis of these rules everybody can enrich the Indonesian language, irrespective of the origin of the newly accepted words. Thus the English words *apple* (Dutch *appel*), *charter, palm, nationalism* (Dutch *nationalisme*) can easily be accepted in Indonesian as *apal, cartar, nasionalisma, palma*.

There still remain the new loan words which consist of three and more syllables, such as *gratifikasi, president, proklamasi, produksi, spekulasi*. If to the word *president* a mute *e* should be added between the *p* and the *r*, it would become a four-syllable word, which is exceptional in Indonesian. It might be advisable in such cases, where the word would have four or more syllables, to ignore the syllabic forms of the Malay language, in order to avoid overlong Indonesian words. Thus such words as *gratifikasi, presiden, proklamasi, produksi, spekulasi* may retain their consonant clusters. Consonant clusters like *nt, nd,* etc., do not occur at the end of words in Indonesian, so the last consonant can easily be omitted.

8. Standardization of vocabulary on an international level

The standardization of the Indonesian vocabulary also has an international aspect. For measures such as *meter, gram,* etc., chemical elements, and formulae etc., it is desirable for the Indonesian language to accept with as little change as possible internationally current words and symbols. Beside, these, however, there is still an abundance of words used by nearly all modern languages of the world, mostly deriving from Graeco-Latin. In becoming a modern language Indonesian will gradually accept more and more concepts of modern culture. If we know that the Indonesian language up until now has coined or accepted more than 500,000 modern terms expressing modern international concepts, we realize that it is moving faster and faster in the direction of a modern language, leaving far behind the other unmodernized Indonesian languages. Since the concepts of science, technology, and other aspects of modern culture are the same or nearly the same in all modern languages, it is of great advantage in learning modern languages and in the exchange of ideas if the Indonesian language accepts words which are similar or nearly similar to those of other modern languages, such as *atom, politik, radio, television, telephone, valuta,* etc. It is obvious that the acceptance of international words by newly standardized languages is of the greatest advantage for the growing world community.[8]

9. The standardization of grammar

The standardization of the rules of grammar of the modern Indonesian language must result in determining a normative grammar accepted by the language community. Such a grammar is first of all necessary for use in schools, since it is primarily the school teacher who must have a standard of correct language usage, which he teaches to his students, and which gradually will be accepted by the whole community.

Perhaps it would have been possible to construct a grammar of the Indonesian language from the standpoint of this language only, to create new categories in order to arrive at a grammar best adapted to the structure and other characteristics of the language. Had this been done, the Indonesian grammar would only have been understandable within the framework of Indonesian or perhaps some other related languages.

Since the Indonesian language is supposed to be a medium of expression and communication in the modern world, it is advisable to write an Indonesian grammar which would describe the structure of the language by means of categories and terms of the grammar of modern languages such as Dutch and English. In this way Indonesian grammar would not lose all contact with modern languages; on the contrary, a bridge could be erected between them, facilitating the learning of these languages by Indonesians and vice versa. But since Indonesian had its own characteristics and categories, of course special attention has to be paid to them.

On various occasions I have indicated that modern linguistics as a whole pays very little attention to the writing of normative grammars, which is understandable, because modern languages are already highly standardized.[9]

The Indonesian language is one among about two hundred and fifty languages belonging to the same language group. The Malay language, as modern Indonesian was called earlier, is not even the largest and most important language of that group. As *lingua franca* of at least a thousand years in an area as large as the whole of Europe or the United States of America, its strength was in its adaptability, its lawlessness; thus everybody expressed himself in that language with a minimum of vocabulary and a minimal knowledge of its rules of grammar. Thus Malay became known as the easiest language in the world to learn.

It is clear that this easiness, this lawlessness, which was a great advantage in the unsophisticated contacts between merchants and travellers in the bazaars and harbours, or between foreigners who happened to meet, would turn out to be of great disadvantage when the language became the national and official language of the country, the medium of instruction in schools, the language of law and official correspondence, etc. Thus the problem of paramount importance was how to change a pidginlike *lingua franca* into a stable, sophisticated national and official modern language which would become the vehicle of modern Indonesian thought and culture. Standardized, prescriptive rules had to be determined for use in schools, by officials, and by the common people. A choice had to be made from among various existing rules, or new rules had to be created: Which of the various rules are better adjusted to the new task of the language as the bearer of new Indonesian thought and culture?

Besides the knowledge of the essential characteristics of the Malay language, knowledge of the general characteristics of related languages in the Indonesian area is also necessary for the writing of a normative grammar. Where ambiguity exists in the usage of the Malay language, general or predominant rules in other related languages could be of great help in reaching a decision on a uniform rule. In the case of Indonesian, it is the general predominant rules of the Western part of the Malay-Polynesian language group that should be considered.

A knowledge of the characteristics of Malay and other languages of the western Malay-Polynesian languages does not, however, suffice for the creation of a normative grammar, since modern Indonesian has still another very important characteristic, expressed by the adjective "modern". Indonesian must also be a *modern* language, expressing modern thought and culture, comparable to English, French, German, etc.

10. What is modernization?

At this point I think I cannot escape the obligation to explain again succinctly my concept of modern thought or modern culture. My basic assumption is that cultural phenomena are uniquely related to human behaviour as a result of the special capacity of the human mind to evaluate his world (which includes himself), in contrast to animal behaviour, which is based on drives and instincts. The human values resulting from this evaluating capacity can be discerned in the *theoretical* value aiming at the identification of things and processes in nature, the *economic* value aiming at their utilization, the *religious* value aiming at the holy, the *aesthetic* value aiming at beauty, the *power* value aiming at power, and the *solidarity* value aiming at solidarity, i.e., love, friendship, etc.[10]

All these values are represented in every culture. The difference among the various cultures throughout history is not that there are cultures without one or more of the six basic values, but that the patterns, the configurations of the six evaluational processes, and thus also of values, are different. On this basis we can divide cultures into two types, namely, progressive cultures, in which the theoretical and economic evaluating capacities dominate, and expressive cultures, in which the religious and aesthetic evaluating capacities dominate.

Viewed from this standpoint, what we have called the modernization process in the countries of Asia is nothing but a change of the overall configuration of the evaluating process of these cultures from an expressive to a progressive culture. Thus the same progressive process which during the last four centuries changed the expressive culture of the Middle Ages in Europe into modern culture has now cast the expressive Asian culture into the throes of rapid social and cultural change, or even of revolution.

From this point of view the description of Riau Malay will not give us the vocabulary or the rules of grammar of modern Indonesian. We have to look for other criteria of modern Indonesian based on other research material.

The problem then turns upon the question: Who are the bearers of modern progressive Indonesian culture and, thus, also of the modern Indonesian language? It is the written language of these people that may be used as the basis for determining the rules of a modern Indonesian grammar. Thus the first task is to make a list of individuals who may be considered the best representatives of modern culture and thus are the best users of the modern language.

Even studying the language of a selected number of intellectuals or of the language of the press, parliament, radio, television and university, will not directly result in a structured set of rules, since even these intellectuals, as well as the press, the parliament, etc., are not using the Indonesian language in a standardized way; compared to the great variations in local dialects, however, the differences in usage in this selected material are small and more manageable.

In the process of formulating rules of grammar from the analysed material, the writer of a modern grammar still has to make various decisions in order to formulate clear rules that will form the structured framework of Indonesian. In various cases the rules of traditional Malay can be accepted without modification, for Indonesian is indeed a continuation of Malay. But since the language has continuously been under the influence of the languages and dialects as well as modern languages, such as, English and Dutch, the investigated material reveals differences in the use of affixes and syntax, as well as word formation and word usage. It is the responsibility of the grammarian to choose as best as he can from among varying, often contradictory, possibilities, in order to arrive at a balanced grammar, attuned to the requirements of modern thought and culture.

11. The characteristics of modern culture

In reflecting on modern culture the following conclusions are relevant:
A. The modern world possesses a system of vocabulary on which modern thought and culture are based.
B. Compared to man in other epochs of history, modern man has various

traits which are more or less related to the characteristics of modern thought and culture.

I wish to formulate these traits as follows:

a. Modern man considers himself a center of activity. With his efforts he is able to change and use nature; he is even able to change his own destiny. This principle I would like to call the *activity* principle.

b. Modern thought is comparatively much more rational and abstract than thought in any other culture in the past. This is not only a result of the importance of scientific, economic, and technological thinking in the modern world, but it is also a part of the very essence of modern society, in which rational and abstract relationships in many respects have replaced the concrete, emotional, face-to-face relations of man in earlier communities. A good example is the rationality and abstractness of modern codified law as compared with customary law in traditional societies. This I call the *rational* and *abstract* principle.

c. Related to the abstractness of modern society is also its *sachlichkeit,* its business acumen.

d. Another important characteristic of modern society is its egalitarianism, in contrast to feudalistic society with its clear-cut social hierarchy. This principle, which I call the *egalitarian* principle, is especially relevant in Indonesia, where the most important language in the archipelago — namely Javanese — is built on the principle of a society with a sophisticated hierarchy. The child must use a second vocabulary when speaking with his parents, as must the common man when addressing a person of higher social rank.

c. Apart from these characteristics of modern thought and culture, the fact is very important that never before has the unity of the world been as great as in our epoch. The rise of new nations with their own languages will to some extent neutralize the advantages of modern means of communication and transportation created by modern science and technology. Consequently we must explore the possibilities of a rapprochement between the modern languages in their spelling, their vocabulary, their syntax, and their morphology. A study of the common features of languages might be very useful. It will only be to the advantage of the modern Indonesian language if it has common elements — for instance in vocabulary, abbreviations, etc. — with the most important modern languages of the world, without losing its own characteristics as the Indonesian language. This advantage is, for example, very clear in the names of the elements and the formulas of chemistry, in the standardization of measurements, and the like.

12. The standardization of the affixes

Speaking about the standardization of grammar in the Indonesian language, we are first of all concerned with the use of the affixes, since the use of the affix is the dominant characteristic of the Indonesian language as an agglutinating language.

In the standardization of the use of the affixes, we face to a certain extent the same problems as in the standardization of the vocabulary. Every uniform use of an affix in a certain function may be considered a form of standardization. However, in the context of language planning or language engineering the aim of standardization must also include the attempt to arrive at the simplest pattern of their usage. Here again we must attempt to acquire the most consistent system of rules, with as few exceptions as possible. Learning the rules of declension in German, for example, becomes in the last analysis learning the manifold exceptions, the same as when learning the conjugation of the French verbs. In this connection a basic analysis of the various Indonesian prefixes is necessary.

Having made this statement we can take the next step in analysing the grammatical features of the Indonesian language. Since we are, to a certain extent, still at the beginning of language planning or language engineering, we must try to formulate some guidelines for maximum consistency and coherence of the grammar, aiming at efficient expression and communication. In order to be able to have a survey of the forces and meanings of the Indonesian affixes, we have to find the basic meanings of the various affixes in Malay. It is clear that in the variety of usage, even in exclusively Malay speaking communities, we gradually discern the basic meaning and usage from the derived usage or even from deviations. These deviations could be the result of foreign influences or misunderstandings. Were they not so widespread and important in language practice, we could discard these deviations as dialectal forms or as substandard. There still remain the derivatives from the e.g., *ber-uang, ber-baju* (to have money, to have clothes). From the basic Indonesian prefix *ber-*, it is very likely that its basic meaning is "to have", e.g. *ber-uang, ber-baju* (to have money, to have clothes). From the basic meaning "to have" it is easy to arrive at the derivative meaning "to use", "to produce", "to be in a situation expressed by the noun", etc. In determining the rules for the basic meaning and the derivative meaning, knowledge of the dialects and other regional Indonesian languages, belonging to the same group as the Malay language, is of great help in making the rules more consistent and coherent.

It is clear that in the description and determination of the usage of a prefix such as *ber-*, an attempt must be made to delineate its difference with the affixes nearest in meaning and form, in this case the prefix *me-*, especially since both of them form the predicate in Indonesian. It could be that the *ber-* and *me-* prefixes formerly were of the same origin, but in the course of history different tendencies were followed, so that at present the difference between the two prefixes is very clear. *Ber-* expresses more: "having" and "being in a situation", while the prefix *me-* creates words which are nearer to the Indo-German active transitive verbs. The comparison of a classical text such as the *Hikayat Seri Rama* and a modern novel such as *Layar Terkembang* shows the clear tendency in modern Indonesian to use more active predicate words with the prefix *me-* than with the prefix *ber-*, which functions more like an adjective. This tendency of the change of the predicate from the description of a situation to the description of an activity runs parallel with the social tendency of the individualization and dynamization of the individual subject in Indonesian culture today through the influence of modern culture. In this line of reasoning a guideline is found for the decision in alternatives, where two predicate words with different prefixes are used for nearly the same function and meaning, e.g., the form *bernyanyi* and *menyanyi* are used in Indonesia to express the same meaning: "to sing". *Menyanyi* is used more and more and is, according to the line of reasoning above, also preferable to *bernyanyi*.

13. The problem of the derivation of loan words

One of the difficult grammatical problems faced in borrowing words from a foreign language is the question: In which grammatical form should foreign words be accepted — in the plural or the singular, as verbs, adjectives, nouns, or in some other form? In the beginning the situation was very confusing. For the word "element", for example, two Arabic forms were used, namely *unsur* and *anasir;* one in the singular and the other in the plural form. Persons using the Arabic plural *anasir* often used the word again in the Indonesian plural by reduplicating it: *anasir-anasir*.

The intellectual who can speak and write Dutch has the tendency to use Dutch words according to Dutch pronunciation and grammatical form. But once a word is used by the common people who do not know Dutch, a new development starts. Let me elucidate this with an example. After the liberation everybody spoke of *proklamasi kemerdekaan*: "the proclamation of independence". But in the sentence "Indonesia proclaimed its independence on August 17, 1945," "proclaimed" is translated into Indonesian as *mem-proklamirkan*, because of the Dutch verb *proclameren.* It is clear that the acceptance of a word both as a verb and a noun will make the Indonesian language needlessly complicated and difficult. The transition from *proklamir* to *proklamasi* will not be understandable in the Indonesian grammar, or the grammar must introduce new affixes. It should be enough to incorporate in the Indonesian language one of the two forms and treat it further in accordance with the rules of Indonesian morphology. Thus it is possible to accept the noun *proklamasi* from the Dutch "proclamatie". But if *proklamasi* is to be used as a verb according to the rules of the Indonesian language, the form "to proclaim" should be *memproklamasi-kan.* It is of course also possible to adapt the verb *proklamir:* the Indonesian noun derived from it should then be *proklamir-an.* It is, however, more or less accepted that for the adaptation of a European word into Indonesian the noun form should be preferred.

More difficult is the problem of the adaptation of a group of European words deriving from the same stem but through affixation representing a great variety of forms and meanings, such as "ratio", "rational", "rationality", "to rationalize", "rationalization", and "rationalism". At present the word *rasio* is accepted as an Indonesian word. The same is true of *rasionalisasi* (from the Dutch: "rationalisatie"); the word "rationalism" can be translated as *serba rasio* or adapted as *rasionalisma,* "to rationalize" is now *merasionalisasi.* For "rational" the common usage is *rasionil* (Dutch "rationeel"), because of the influence of the Dutch pronunciation. Should *rasio, rasionalisasi* and *rasionil* be accepted as separate, isolated words, or should new suffixes be introduced in the Indonesian grammar, borrowed from Graeco-Latin or modern languages, in order that the relationship between these three words becomes understandable in Indonesian? The latter will have many consequences, and would only be advisable if the necessary introduction of new suffixes really has a chance of being less complicated. I am of the opinion that a more satisfactory system would be achieved by attempting to withdraw from Indonesian the form *rasionil* or *rasional* and replacing it by an Indonesian prefixation *berasio,* meaning "having ratio". The word *rasionil* or *rasional* is already so popular that at the moment there is little chance that *berasio* will be able to take its place soon.

14. Abstract concepts

Another guideline is needed for expressing abstract concepts in Indonesian. Compared with the old Malay language, modern Indonesian uses many more abstract concepts such as *kebangsaan* (nationality), *kebenaran* (truth), *kebanggaan* (pride), etc., which arose clearly under the influence of modern thought, which is more abstract than the old Indonesian way of thinking. The modern Indonesian language expresses these abstract concepts by means of the prefix *ke-* in combination with the suffix *-an.* There was a time when the translation *Minumlah obat untuk kesehatanmu* of the Dutch sentence "Neem medicijn voor je gezondheid" ("take medicine for your health") was not acceptable, because it was considered a too literal translation from Dutch.

According to traditional Malay rules and thoughts the Indonesian sentence should be *Minumlah obat supaya engkau menjadi sehat* ("take medicine in order that you become healthy"). The decision for the standardization of modern Indonesian should accept this new grammatical form expressing new abstract concepts and the logic of modern thought.

The breakthrough of abstract modern thought in the Indonesian language is clearly expressed in the decline of classificatory numerals like *buah* for round things, *batang* for elongated things, *ekor* for animals, etc. Where the correct usage of numerals in the Malay language indicates the number of objects and animals by classificatory numerals, such as *sebuah telur* [one (fruit) egg], *sebatang rokok* [one (stem) cigarette], *dua ekor anjing* [two (tail) dog], in modern Indonesian these classificatory numerals are used less and less frequently. The numerals themselves are already considered sufficient in English: "an or one egg, a or one cigarette, two dogs", which are nowadays frequently translated as *satu telur, satu rokok, dua anjing.* It is in the context of abstract modern thinking that we can accept this new grammatical form of the numerals.

The crisis in the use of pronouns reflects the change in social relationship. The old pre-Hindu native Indonesian languages have a great variety of pronouns, especially of the second and third person, expressing the dominant position of the family relationship of its social structure. People of the same age or of the same family line as one's mother and father, are also called *ibu* ("mother") and *bapak* ("father"), while people of the same generation are called *kakak* if they are older, or *adik* if they are younger.

During the Hindu epoch of Indonesian history the hierarchical system of feudalism expressed itself in a system of pronouns differentiated according to the hierarchy of status and age of the speaker, the adressed, or the third person. The lower in status or in age has to use the more modest and refined pronouns in addressing an older person or one of higher status. This fact is, for example, clearly discernible in the Javanese language, where other words are also classified according to low, middle, and higher language forms. Even today the usage of pronouns is still not sufficiently standardized. For the first person singular the word *saya* is used more and more, for the plural *kami* and *kita*, the first excluding the addressed, the second including the addressed. The word *aku* is used in more intimate relationships. For the second person singular *kumu* and *engkau* is used, comparable to "tu" in French and 'du' in German, further *tuan* ("gentleman"), *nyonya* ("Mrs."), *nona* ("Miss"); while in the plural *sekalian* is added. The national movement in this century has made popular the democratic word *saudara* ("brother"), but since independence *bapak* ("father") and *ibu* ("mother") are used more and more in addressing older persons or persons of a higher status. More in line with a democratic attitude is the word *anda*, which was coined two decades ago. Gradually this word has dominated the sphere of advertisement, announcements, and other abstract relationships with the public. During the last few years it also started to be used in radio and television, and sometimes in official correspondence. It is very likely that the word *anda* will be the future standardized form of the Indonesian second person, comparable to the English *you*. The third person is more standardized in the forms *dia* (singular) and *mereka* (plural). Sometimes *beliau* is used, to express respect for older persons or a person of higher status.

15. The change in syntax

As a consequence of the absence of declension and conjugation, Indonesian syntax is dominated by word order and accentuation of the words in the sentence. The rule of Indonesian word order is that the following word determines the previous one. In conformity with this rule the predicate comes after the subject, the adjective after the noun.[11]

Even in a compound, the second element determines the first. In the meaning of a sentence the word order can be changed by the accentuation of the sentence. In this case inversion can also take place. In determining a new standardized word order, the problem is to what extent the influence of the more dynamic European languages can be accepted in the rather rigid system of Malay word order. Dutch, which had a strong influence on the educated younger generation of the first half of this century, shows more freedom in the placing of the adverb or adverbial phrase than does Indonesian. The increase of the use of Indonesian by Dutch-educated intellectuals tends to make the Indonesian sentence more variegated and flexible in word order.

16. The perspective of the unification and standardization of the Indonesian and Malaysian language

It will be to the advantage of both the Indonesian and Malaysian language if standardization of spelling, grammar, and vocabulary can be achieved as soon as possible along with a cooperation in the production of books, encyclopedias, and other materials. A common language institution would surely work to the advantage of both participating countries.

The efforts at a common spelling date from the 17th of April 1959, when Malaya or the Persekutuan Tanah Melayu came to an agreement with the Republic of Indonesia.

In December of the same year, a discussion took place between the Malayan and Indonesian Committees for a common spelling in the Latin script, called the Melindo spelling. This spelling should have been announced in January 1962, but political difficulties between the two countries in the following years prevented the realization of the Melindo spelling. After the end of the political confrontation, the committees of both countries came to a new agreement on common spelling, which should have been proclaimed in Indonesia during its fortieth celebration of the pledge of the Indonesian Youth on October 28, 1968. Public resistance against the new spelling, however, was so strong that its announcement had to be postponed again.

At long last, after various deliberations in a better political atmosphere the new common spelling was announced at the Indonesian Independence Anniversary by the President of Indonesia on August 17, 1972, while an announcement by the Malaysian government also took place on the same date. After the proclamation of a common spelling for the Indonesian and Malaysian language, the most urgent problem is the coordination or unification of modern terminology and grammar for both languages.

It is encouraging to see that the newly published Malaysian dictionary, the *Kamus Dewan* by Dr. Teuku Iskandar in Kuala Lumpur, has included all Indonesian words of the Indonesian dictionaries *Kamus Umum Bahasa Indonesia* by W.J.S. Poerwadarminta and the *Kamus Moderen Bahasa Indonesia* by S. M. Zain, so that it is now the most complete dictionary of the Indonesian-Malaysian language.

I have emphasized the coordination and standardization of the Indonesian and Malaysian languages here, because I am convinced that the importance of a language, to a great extent, depends on the number of speakers of that language. A language with a greater number of speakers has greater potentialities for development and progress than a smaller one. With the Malaysian language and the Malay language of Singapore and Brunei, the Indonesian/ Malaysian language will be the fifth-largest language in the world, used by about 170,000,000 people. If we remember that the same language is also spoken in the southern part of Thailand and even in some parts of the Philippines, its position is even stronger.

The UNESCO project for the study of Malay culture, which is supported not only by Malaysia, Indonesia, and the Philippines but also by Singapore, Thailand, Cambodia, Laos, and Vietnam, even Madagascar, will undoubtedly give to the Indonesian/Malaysian language the chance to play, in the future, an even more important role in the whole of South-East Asia. The Indonesian/

Malaysian language is the most important language of the Malay-Polynesian
group which has the opportunity to become a large, mature language in the
modern world. In this connection I should like to mention that in Australia
the Indonesian language is already being offered to students at high schools
and in some places even at primary schools.

It is to be hoped that the Indonesian government will take the initiative
and also the leadership in the coordination and standardization of the Indonesian and Malaysian language for the advantage of both countries and the
whole of South-East Asia.[12]

Notes

1 Baugh 1956: 313.
2 Ibid. 314.
3 Leonard 1962: 12.
4 Alisjahbana 1969: 56–69.
5 Cf. Downing 1962, Wijk 1959.
6 Brandstetter 1910.
7 Dempwolff 1934–1938.
8 Cf. Sudarno.
9 See my inaugural lecture delivered at the University of Malaya: *The failure of modern
linguistics in the face of linguistic problems of the twentieth century.* Kuala Lumpur,
University of Malaya, 1965.
10 For further elaboration of this value theory in relation to cultural phenomena, see
Alisjahbana 1966.
11 There are several exceptions to this rule, such as the position of numeral adjectives
before nouns, etc.
12 For a survey of the problems of language engineering in connection with the modernization and standardization of Indonesian, see Alisjahbana 1976.

References

Alisjahbana, S. Takdir 1966. *Values as integrating forces in personality, society and
culture.* Kuala Lumpur: University of Malaya Press.
Alisjahbana, S. Takdir 1969. *Indonesia: social and cultural revolution.* Kuala Lumpur
etc.: Oxford University Press.
Alisjahbana, S. Takdir 1976. *Language planning for modernization: the case of Indonesian
and Malaysian.* The Hague: Mouton.
Baugh, Albert C. 1956. *A history of the English language.* London: Routledge and Kegan
Paul.
Brandstetter, R. 1910. *Wurzel und Wort in den indonesischen Sprachen.* (Monographien
zur Indonesischen Sprache VI). Luzern.
Dempwolff, O. 1934–1938. Vergleichende Lautlehre des Austronesischen Wortschatzes.
Zeitschrift für Eingeborenen-Sprachen XV, XVII, XIX, Beihefte.
Downing, J. A. 1962. *To be or not to be. The augmented Roman alphabet.* London.
Leonard, Sterling A. 1962. *The doctrine of correctness in English usage, 1700–1800.*
New York.
Sudarno (n. d.) *Persoalan bunyi dan tatabunyi bahasa Indonesia serta usaha pembakuan-
nya* (mimeo.).
Wijk, A. 1959. *Regularized English.* Stockholm.

Linguistic minorities and national languages

R. N. SRIVASTAVA, *UNIVERSITY OF DELHI*

This paper has a mainly theoretical and definitional character. I will try to understand two of the critical terms of the topic of our task-force meeting, viz., *Linguistic Minority* and *National Language*. This I consider vital for three reasons: (a) such linguistic terms reflect the process by which we deal cognitively with our sociocultural reality and thus tend to differ in their extensional and intensional meanings across societies; (b) defining criteria for these terms drawn under the pressure of monolingual experience show a poor understanding of our multilingual ethos (Pattanayak 1981; Srivastava 1982); and (c) there is a resurgence of ethnic-minority nationalism all over the world, and minorities have given up their passive existence and are showing signs of militant assertion. While this resurgence is leading to "retribalization" in the interests of decentrality in the First World (Anderson 1981), in Third World countries it is coming into conflict with the process of "detribalization" as a prerequisite for national unity.

Literally speaking, the term *minority* stands for the smaller in number of two aggregates that together constitute a whole. However, this statistical definition of *minority* neither tells anything about the social status of a minority group vis-à-vis the majority group in a given society, nor does it reflect its attitude towards the majority group and vice-versa. Secondly, it talks about only two aggregates, neglecting thus a situation in which there may be more than two constituents which together form a composite whole. For example, India attests the existence of at least twelve major languages, but none of them is spoken by more than half of the 600 million of the total population. Should we characterize India then as a country of only linguistic minorities? Thirdly, such a definition of minority can include in its orbit even that elite and dominant section of society which, in spite of being far smaller in number, happens to wield power and has access to resources which are not available to the subordinate but majority group population. For example, according to the 1971 census, less than 3 % of the total population of India have claimed English as their mothertongue, yet it is this elite group which is the most privileged and powerful section of the society.

There is yet another perspective through which the semantics of the term *linguistic minority* has been circumscribed. This perspective introduces first the notion of "language power" based on the following three criteria: (a) the wider action radius and range of usage in a certain domain; (b) greater degree of control over the speakers of another language, and (c) higher status and prestige in the eyes of the people (Pieterson 1978).Language power brings out the dichotomy of dominant [+ power] versus dominated [− power]. According to Haugen, "a common euphemism for a dominated group was a *minority* group, and we might very well speak of minority languages even though their speakers were in some areas in actual majority" (Haugen 1978 : 11). Such a definition obliterates the distinction between the general mass (*Janta*) and ethnic or linguistic minorities. Janta is not, in a real sense, a minority group. We have to distinguish the cases of Janta movement from those of the active separatist movements of ethnic minorities. The Janta movement has during the past half century brought into the family of nations a number of new members who were formerly colonies of Western powers. With their political independence, these nations are now referred to as developing countries. While Janta movement is a movement of a numerically characterized majority group against the domination of the elitist minority group, the resurgence of ethnic movements all over the world is due to the struggle of minority groups against the dominant majority groups for maintaining boundaries for their linguistic or ethnic survival. It is for this reason that a minority is defined as a group held together whose race or language is different from that of the majority of inhabitants of a given society. Within developing nations we find at least two distinct types of minority groups − one which is gradually losing its cultural and ethnic distinctiveness and, hence, is in the process of changing ethnic identification, and another which, after reaching a state of crisis in its struggle, has become militant in orientation.

The above discussion makes it imperative to delimit the semantics of the term *minority* by taking simultaneously two variables − one related to *Quantum* dimension and the other related to *Power* dimension. In the quantum dimension, these two variables provide fourfold categories:

	+ Power −	
+	(A) Majority	(B) Janta
−	(C) Elite	(D) Minority

Quantum

We would like to restrict the semantics of the term *minority* to a group which in a given polity or region functions with a feature complex [− Quantum, − Power], i.e., which falls under our category (D), as opposed to *majority*, which as a group exhibits the feature complex [+ Quantum, + Power]. The *Janta Group* displays the feature complex [+ Quantum, − Power], which is just the opposite of the feature value of the *Elite Group* manifested by the complex [− Quantum, + Power]. This can be well exemplified by the language scene we have in the two Union territories of our country − Dadar and Nagar Haveli and Goa, Daman, and Diu. In the former case, Bhili, a tribal speech community, represents 83.1 % of the total population, while in the latter case the territory is occupied by 64.86 % of Konkani speakers. But in spite of their statistical majority, they do not enjoy the status of official languages. English enjoys in both the Union territories the status of official language [+ Power], though its speakers are numerically the most insignificant ones.

For an operational definition of *minority*, the question of Quantum takes on some other dimensions of complexity. If minority group means a social group which is numerically less than 50 %, then an additional query has to be raised, namely, 50 % of what? This question was taken up by the Supreme Court of India at the time when the Kerala Education Bill (passed on 2 September 1957 by the Legislative Assembly) was referred back to it by the President of India under Art. 200 of the Indian Constitution. The Supreme Court rejected the stand of the Government of Kerala, which proposed to define the concept of minority statistically, by restricting the region in which the educational institution in question was situated. The Supreme Court raised a very pertinent question: "If for the implementation of a State Law a part of the State is to be accepted, then what should the size of the part be − a district or a subdivision or a *taluk* or a town or its suburbs or a municipality or its wards?" It held the view that if a Bill is passed by a State Legislature, the minority must be determined in the context of the entire population of the State for which the Law is enacted. Consequently, for the purposes of the Act of the Union Government, the term *minority* must be operationally defined in the context of the total population of India. Such an operational definition makes the concept of *minority* in India a relative term, dependent upon the nature and size of the administrative region in which minority groups are situated.

The concept of *minority group* must not be confused with the notion of *minor language* and its users. It is true that in general, users of a minor language in a given society form a group which in its manifestation is either Janta or Minority. But this is not necessarily the case in the plurilingual context of India. We find instances where speakers of a "major" language are socially oppressed and economically impoverished simply because they are singled out from the majority group for differential and unequal treatment. It is to be remembered that the concept of "minor" language is based on the evolutionary perspective of languages which classifies languages in certain sociolinguistic types: for example, minor (undeveloped), early modern (developing), modern (developed) contemporary etc. (Hymes 1972; Neustupný 1974). This concept should be carefully distinguished from the concept of "minority" language which simply means a language – developed or undeveloped – employed by users who in a given situation are numerically and/or functionally in the minority, i.e., as a group who are qualified by the feature complex [– Quantum, – Power]. Thus, we may find a "major" language whose speakers are minority in status in spite of the fact that in linguistic configuration it is a relatively developed one: for example, Telugu in Delhi or in Tamilnadu. In such cases a minority language of one region is the language of the majority in some other region. In most such cases, language itself does not become automatically a crucial index of speakers' status-inferiority. Contrary to this, "inferiority" of "minor" languages automatically gets imposed on the users of that language.

What is not to be lost sight of is the fact that, in the sense the term "minority" is being used here, it designates a social group which apart from being socially oppressed is an object of collective discrimination. In the case of the users of a "minor" language, language itself is made a cause and excuse for their status inferiority. There is a tendency to consider them as tribals, uncultivated, rustics, etc., because their languages, in structure and function, are underdeveloped. Nothing of this sort happens where the speakers of a "major" language gain statistically a minority status in some region. Sanskrit is a major language whose speakers are insignificant in quantum, but its use never became an index of speakers' statusinferiority. Similarly, Tamilians and Gujaratis in Maharashtra or Telugu and Marathi speakers in Karnataka, though statistically in a minority, are not looked upon as uncultivated or rustics.

Keeping in view the distinction between major/minor languages (descriptive of the language itself) and majority/minority languages (descriptive of its social status and function), we find at least the following types of Linguistic Minorities in India:

(A) A major (developed) language whose speakers are in minority with a feature complex
      (a) [− Quantum, + Power], e.g., English/Hindi in India,
      (b) [− Quantum, − Power], e.g., Telugu in Tamilnadu,
      (c) [+ Quantum, − Power], e.g., Kashmiri in Jammu and Kashmir.
(B) A minor (underdeveloped) language whose speakers are in minority with a feature complex
      (d) [+ Quantum, − Power], e.g., Bhili in Dadar and Nagar Haveli territory, and
      (e) [− Quantum, − Power], e.g., Santal and Kurux in Bihar.

The present typology suggests convincingly that the concept of linguistic minority in the multilingual setting of India is a relative term. It also shows that the (a) type is not in fact a true instance of linguistic minority because their members neither live under social oppression, nor do they regard themselves as objects of collective discrimination. Contrary to this, the (e) type is the exemplary instance of linguistic minority as, it is members of this type who are economically impoverished, politically oppressed and, socially differentiated for unequal treatment. Consequently, it is this class whose members develop in themselves a cluster of negative attitudes and begin to regard themselves as objects of collective discrimination.

Not only is the concept of minority in India and other multilingual and multiethnic countries of Asia and Africa a relative term, but in certain contexts it also becomes sociopolitical in orientation. For example, on the recommendation of the States Reorganization Commission, boundaries of certain states in India were redrawn on a linguistic basis in 1956. Behind the scheme was the idea of bringing together people speaking a common language. The Commission thought that thus it would reduce the number of linguistic minorities and, consequently, also reduce the problems of minorities. But the reorganization of states on a linguistic basis could neither reduce the number nor solve all the problems of linguistic minorities. In fact, it transformed the discontented and agitating minority community into a majority group by giving it absolute majority in the statistical sense. In doing so, it tried to change the very nature of our society. Historically, social and ethnic factors made different speech communities in India coexist peacefully, giving rise to a nonconflicting type of societal bilingualism. But the States Reorganization Commission, by bringing together people speaking a common language, on the one hand developed a tendency among members of different speech communities to live in geographically circumscribed regions and, on the other hand, generated a sense of isolationism and separatism in the members of different speech communities. All this helped to create a competing and conflicting type of isolated bilingualism from within a society which has been basically noncompeting and nonconflicting in character since prehistoric times (Srivastava 1981).

The fact that the reorganization of states on a linguistic basis could solve only the problem of linguistic majority groups rather than any problem of linguistic minorities may be seen from the effect the scheme of redistribution of state boundaries has had on our Indian polity and society. In 1956, there were only 16 states, whereas in 1971 the Indian Union consisted of 22 linguistically organized[1] States and 9 Union Territories.

The process of bifurcation of States has some relevance to the study of the nature of majority and minority groups and the shift in their mutual relationship. Maharashtra was bifurcated in 1960 into two states because of the two prominent speech communities, Gujarati and Marathi, and in 1966 Punjab was divided into two states — Punjabi Suba and Haryana — because of the conflict between two religious groups, Hindus and Sikhs, the former adhering to Hindi and the latter to Punjabi.

Before this division[2] the, Sikh population in Punjab was a minority, as is shown by the 1961 Census. It was in fact 33.33 % of the total population of the State. After the reorganization, the Sikh population in Punjab rose to 60.22 %, as is revealed by the 1971 Census. Sikhs as a religious group now became the dominant majority. The case has been similar with the Punjabi and Hindi languages. The following table speaks for itself:

HINDI-PUNJABI IN PUNJAB

1961		1971	
Hindi	Punjabi	Hindi	Punjabi
55.6	41.1	20.01	79.49

What was in 1961 a "minority" in the Punjab State became a "majority" in 1971 and vice-versa as far as Hindi and Punjabi languages are concerned. This type of situation developed wherever the redistribution of state territories took place. By creating Punjabi Suba the discrimination against one of the three prominent but minority religious communities of India — Muslims, Christians, and Sikhs — might have been done away with, but, in the process, it created there out of a majority another minority community, i.e., Hindus. Thus, the problem of minority remained, because this problem is *sui generis*.

All these facts simply show that linguistic reorganization of states in itself is no solution to our vital problem of linguistic minorities. The fact must not be lost sight of that different states might have been declared uni- or bilingual for administrative convenience, but basically each one of them is a multi-lingual and pluricultural entity. "There is not a single State in the country which is completely unilingual; not a single major modern Indian language whose speakers do not employ at least three contact languages; and not a single speech community which has less than at least three distinct linguistic codes in its verbal repertoire. We find all major languages of India existing beyond their home-territory; almost all regions like cosmopolitan cities, show culturally a mixed population" (Srivastava 1980: 13—14).

As reorganization of States was based on the principle of bringing about a condition in the territory favorable for the promotion of one or two languages to dominant position, it also created a setting for a new dimension of conflict and tension between two or more speech communities who had once enjoyed peaceful coexistence. This is aptly reflected in the First Report of the Commissioner for Linguistic Minorities: "The division of the states on linguistic basis has given rise to the inevitable result that the regional language should gain prominence and should in course of time become the official language of the State. The other languages which are the mother-tongue of the minority communities living in the State, naturally do not get equal prominence or status. The result is that those whose mother-tongue is the minority language have not only a sentimental grievance but certain practical difficulties and inconveniences from which they suffer" (First Report: 44). The recent state-wide linguistic violence which took place in the month of April, 1982, in Karnataka over the Gokak Committee Report is a clear reflection of the suffering of minorities and, their sentimental grievances. Karnataka is a southern state in which Kannada enjoys all dominant status with 65.97 % of speakers. Urdu and Telugu, with 9.00 % and 8.18 % of speakers respectively are the next two numerically significant minority groups. The primary demand of the dominant speech community was to accept the report which recommended that Kannada be the exclusive first language in the school education under the Three Language Formula. All of the pro-Report agitators cried: "We shall lay down our lives for Kannada". The Urdu minority group took up cudgels against the report and got support from other linguistic minority groups — Telugu, Marathi, Hindi, Tamil, etc. It was as the result of sharp criticism by linguistic minorities that a proposal was finally accepted which suggested that Kannada for Kannadigas and the respective mothertongues for the speakers of Urdu, Telugu, Tamil, Marathi, Hindi and English should be the first language, and that Kannada, the state official language, should be made compulsory as a second language for non-Kannada speakers.

As to the question "what happens if none of the speech communities in a given polity is numerically more than 50 % of its total population?" the answer is that the fourfold distinction, i.e., majority group, Janta group, elite group and minority group, is not to be taken either as absolute or as inevitable. For example, in spite of the fact that Hindi is spoken by less than 50 % of the total population of India, it has been accorded the position of official language of the Union. Thus, on the quantum dimension, the Hindi speech community cannot claim to be a majority group because its native speakers do not have the requisite number to qualify for the feature, [+ Quantum]. But this is so for the other twelve principal speech communities of India as well. We have to remember that the federal structure of India, with 22 states and 9 Union territories, is dominated by 12 speech communities where each such community, with its language, enjoys certain dominance in the spheres of public interaction. But in a multilingual country with a strong tradition of its own, this dominance [+ Power] comes more from the functionality of a language than the status officially assigned to it by the polity.

As India's language scene offers multiplicity of languages with concentric bilingualism, we find the domain of national languages multilayered and multifunctional. For example, Hindi serves as a majority language in six states with the following percentages: Rajasthan (91.13), Haryana (89.42), Uttar Pradesh (88.54), Himachal Pradesh (86.87), Madhya Pradesh (83.3), and Bihar (79.77), as well as in two Union territories — Delhi (75.97) and Chandigarh (55.96). But mother-tongue speakers of Hindi have spilled over into neighbouring states and beyond. For example, it is the numerically second most important language in the Punjab (20.01) and West Bengal (6.13) and is third in number in no less than five states — Jammu and Kashmir, Assam, Maharashtra, Andhra Pradesh, and Tripura. What we notice is that Hindi as a contact language is spoken by more than one-third of the entire bilingual population and takes on the communicative load on the all-India scene. It is not the quantum of mother-tongue speakers of Hindi (which is 38.06 % of the total population of India) which makes it a viable force; it is rather concentric bilingualism with Hindi as a contact language which provides it with imperceptible strength. The nature and extent of concentric bilingualism proposes a hypothesis that the percentage of bilingualism among the the speakers is lower for that language which has higher functional potential value for cross-regional speech interaction, i.e., lingua-franca (Srivastava 1977: 78). Thus we have the mean percentage of bilingualism for the four categories (Apte 1970: 72).

Category	1. Hindi	5.105
	2. Major State Languages	9.569
	3. Major Non-State Languages	18.842
	4. Minor Language	42.144

As Glyn Lewis points out for the Soviet Union as well, high levels of bilingualism characterize the small national groups, especially if they are in the minority within larger linguistic communities (Lewis 1972: 46).

The above discussion leads us to the conclusion that the ratio of bilingualism for a given language of India is in inverse proportion to the functional value of that language as a means of wider communication, and that in India this functional value is relative and scaled (rather than absolute, as rates of bilingualism for the four categories reveal). If so, the power dimension for characterizing Major/Minority groups should also be given a concentric orientation. It is this concentric orientation that has kept India integrated into one composite whole.

If we look at the different policies which various minority groups adopt in response to their subordinate position, we find them divided mainly into two groups: (1) those policies which tend toward integration, and (2) those which tend toward conflict. Integration policies can be further divided into two: (1a) *pluralist,* wherein a minority group is allowed to retain its cultural and linguistic identity, thus giving rise to the situation of linguistic pluralism, and (1b) *assimilationist,* wherein a minority group is encouraged to lose its linguistic identity, thus creating a melting-pot situation in which a minority group adopts the language of the majority superordinates. Similarly, policies which generate conflict can be subdivided into two: (2a) *secessionist,* wherein based on antagonism, a minority group fans its passion of linguistic exclusiveness, and (2b) *militant,* wherein a minority group strives to gain control over the dominant majority and, in the process, tries to extend its linguistic sphere of influence.

It should be noted that India has been multilingual for several millennia. Its basic characteristic has been the allocation of social roles to different languages. As a result, it has sustained a nonconflicting type of societal bilingualism. Implicit in it has been the pluralist policy which encouraged linguistic minorities to retain their cultural distinctiveness. But with the formation of regional linguistic states a few of the languages were raised to the status of regional official languages. This blocked the social mobility of the members of speech communities which are characterized by the feature [− Power]. This in turn brought about a change in the orientation in policies which linguistic minorities as a group adopted in response to their oppressed condition. We find on the Indian scene an attempt being made by ethnolinguistic minorities to gain autonomy or to assert their ethnic identity through the revival of their language.

We notice that in the recent past there have been many kinds of language movements by linguistic minorities. The situation has become acute because the question of role allocation for different linguistic codes has been politicized. "Linguistic diversity has existed in India from the beginning of her recorded history. What is new and significant for political study is the mobilization of language groups for social and political objectives. These processes of mobilization invariably result in the political restructuring of forces in the Indian society" (Das Gupta 1970: 70).

We find the political expression of language loyalities in different forms of language movements. In order to understand their true nature one has to look, on the one hand, at the nature and functioning of societal bilingualism which India has evolved through its history and, on the other hand, at the state policies concerning ethnolinguistic minorities it is promoting. The state policy of India is not *negative* to minorities, i.e., it is not a policy of annihilation or explicit assimilation. There are a number of constitutional safeguards against the expulsion of ethnolinguistic minorities. But while in the past it had *liberal* orientation (i.e., ethnic federalism which recognizes in some way or other some autonomy for ethnolinguistic minorities), at present it has moved towards a *strong* position of centralization for creation of national unity. With strong and dominant central control it began promoting the process of detribalization as a prerequisite for creation of national integration and unity. In doing so, it relied more on dominant majority languages on the basis of which it tried to carve out different (linguistically demarcated) state boundaries. Thus we find in the Hindi belt different language movements led by different speech communities whose linguistic codes were given, till now, the status of regional dialects of a language. Movements of this kind find expression in the demand for separate states, i.e., the creation of Bhojpur, Vishal Haryana, and Bundelkhand. According to the protagonists of these movements, the existing state boundaries drawn on the basis of dominant languages, are artificial because they cut across linguistic boundaries of linguistic minorities. For example, speakers of Bhojpuri (a regional dialect of Hindi) are spread across Uttar Pradesh and Bihar, speakers of the Bundeli dialect are in Uttar Pradesh and Madhya Pradesh, and speakers of Haryanvi are found in three states, Haryana, Uttar Pradesh and Delhi (Misra 1979).

Another kind of language movement finds expression in establishing and creating common symbols of their regionally marked linguistic identity. For example, adherents of the Maithili or Konkani movement raised their voice on the one hand, against the discriminatory allocation of the roles for their language in administration, education, etc., while, on the other hand calling for the standardization and modernization of their dialects.

The Santali language movement can be said to characterize the third type. The Santals are tribals who, as a linguistic minority, are spread in Bihar, Orissa, Assam, and West Bengal. While the majority superordinates want to impose their own dominant language of the region (Hindi in Bihar, Oriya in Orissa, etc.) and in this attempt at detribalization expect the Santals to give up their tribal traits, the subordinate Santals as a group have decided to create a "great tradition" of their own. The movement is meant to create and perpetuate new cultural and linguistic markers to defend the survival of the tribe against assimilation and absorption.

The case of Indian societal bilingualism refutes the concept of society being composed of discrete groups with a single identity. It also refutes the idea of individuals having a single language as a marker of their sociocultural identity. It shows at least two points of divergence from the simplistic notion of language identity: First, lingua franca may also become a source of identity thereby creating an identity of intergroup (collection of groups) consolidation forming their own sociocultural institutions. For example, Hindi is a lingua franca for the speakers of its several regional dialects, but in terms of a historically established and culturally defined speech community, different dialect speakers of Hindi as an intergroup show certain common distinctive sociopsychological traits and some awareness of their common social identity. Second, in a traditional and stratified society such as that of India, one finds a complex network of hierarchically organized social identities. Consequently, language identities are also layered with a thread of integration.

We find at present the mobilization of language groups for social and political objectives at different layers of our verbal organization, because language conflict may manifest a clash of interest between any two levels of loyalities and identities. For example, language movements against Hindi illustrate the conflict on the following levels: (a) as a language of national communication, it comes into conflict with English, which is recognized as an associate official language of the Union; (b) as a developed (inter-) regional language at the state level it comes into conflict with Tamil, Bengali, etc.; (c) as a lingua franca for its own dialects, it comes into conflict with Maithili, Bhojpuri, etc.; (d) as an alternate literary variant it comes into conflict with Urdu; and (e) as an interethnic link language, it comes into conflict with Santali, Khasi, etc.

All these instances of language movements suggest that language planning and planning of identities for linguistic minorities in the multilingual and pluricultural setting of India is a complex undertaking in which considerable care has to be taken at the levels of policy decisions (fixing of goals and objectives) and policy implementation (execution of plans).

It is true that more resources are being mobilized to legitimize languages in order to integrate India politically and socioculturally. Conscious planning has gone into interlinking various definable and clearly recognizable speech groups with conflicting aspirations, so that they may work more efficiently as one nation-state. However, the concept of *national language* which is being promoted to achieve this goal is not as simple as is generally believed. Before we tackle the problem of characterizing the functional relevance of the concept, it is necessary for us to come to a clear understanding of certain other terms like *nation, nationality,* and *nationism.*

This is vital because one of the pivotal functions of a national language is to integrate the people of a given nation in the form of a stable community of language, territory, economic life, and psychological make-up manifested in a community of culture. However, we should differentiate between the perspectives in which a nation as a polity (i.e., politicoterritorial entity) strives for administrative cohesion and political consolidation and as an *ethnos* (i.e., sociocultural entity) promotes the cause of unity and integration despite rich diversity of cultural inheritance. Our understanding of this difference is vital, because languages play different types of roles in these two distinct contexts. Furthermore, there are nations which have legitimized a single language to subserve both the functions and there are also nations which, through their policy decisions, have tried to legitimize two or more languages for these two distinctive perspectives.

Nation as a polity is based on the notion of state affiliation, political integration, and economic consolidation. It is also marked by a geographically defined sense of identity. This vehicular consciousness for integrating a nation with a view to administrative consolidation and economic growth has been called *Nationism* (Fishman 1969).

Nation as an ethnos is based on the notion of ethnocentrism and the concept of sociocultural authenticity. Like nations as a polity (which may be composed of two or more than two state (province) level administrative institutions), nations as ethnos can also consist of lower level of ethnic or sociocultural institutions, termed *nationalities.* We can note that a nation may be uniethnic like Japan or multiethnic like India. For its socioethnic identity, a nation seeks a superordinate ideologized sentience — commonly termed *Nationalism.* Nationalism serves a unique function — it unifies and ideologizes nationalities in a multiethnic nation. The ideologized dynamism of nationalism is tied down with sociocultural authenticity and tradition. It involves consciousness at the level of nation in form and function of ethnic integration and cultural intensification.

A language called upon to serve the function of nationalism is labeled *National language,* and when employed to achieve the end of nationism is designated *official language*. As conceived in our Constitution, India as a polity is bilingual, with Hindi as the primary and English as an associate official language. As a socioethnic entity, it is multilingual because almost all major regional languages have come to be acknowledged generally as "national" languages of India due to their resilience and vogue. It is to be noted that English is a pan-Indian language. Nevertheless, its promotion to official status as a language of the Union Government of India is motivated by nationism (rather than nationalism). At the same time, nowhere in our Constitution has Hindi been designated as an exclusive national language, though Art. 343 of our Constitution gives Hindi the status of primary official language of the Union and Art. 351 epitomizes the direction of its development for all-India use.

It is true that all major regional languages of India integrate their speech communities socio-culturally and in this respect perform a role similar to that of Hindi in its own region, where it is a state official language. Thus, there are people who claim that in terms of antiquity, amplitude, opulence, resilience, and current vitality, languages such as Bengali, Marathi, Tamil, Telugu, etc., too claim parity with Hindi (Iyengar 1973). Consequently, we notice that almost all major regional languages are to some extent contributing positively towards the integration of Indian speech communities. However, it is also being felt that India needs a language that could symbolize sentience of nationalism for the purpose of integrating different nationalities at the pan-Indian level.

What is important to observe is that in multilingual countries of the Third World, national language, nationality languages, and minority languages form a linguistic continuum: national language at the one end and "in-group" minority languages at the other end, with an intersecting middle zone of major, mediate and minor types of nationality languages. This linear aspect of language continuum in the context of the Indian situation attests at least the following language-types:

(i)   *National/Official Language,* i.e., interlanguage for languages of "great tradition"; for example, Hindi in pan-Indian context,

(ii)   *Major Nationality Languages,* i.e., interlanguage for languages of "little tradition"; for example, Bengali, Marathi, Tamil, Telugu, etc.

(iii) *Mediate Nationality Languages,* i.e., linguistic minorities in search of their own "great tradition"; for example, Santali, Konkani, etc.

(iv)   *"Out-group" Minority Languages,* i.e., linguistic minorities with "little tradition" serving also as languages of wider communication; for example, Halbi, Sadari, etc., and

(v)   *"In-group" Minority Languages,* i.e., linguistic minorities with
      "little tradition" serving exclusively the function of intragroup
      communication; for example, Mishing in Assam, Malto in Bihar, or
      Juang in Orissa.

The distinction between national, nationality, and minority languages
should be seen in the wider perspective of their assigned roles in the overall
communication setting and central educational policy of a given country. In
fact, the Education Commission of India tried to encapsulate the notion of
language continuum in its Three Language Formula for school education.
This Formula suggests that while English, Hindi, and other major nationality
languages should be used in secondary and primary education, minor minority languages may be used in primary education.

It is true that literacy is most effectively achieved in the mothertongue. It is
equally true that mothertongue literacy allows everyone an equal access to educational opportunities. But on the level of policy implementation, there seem
to be a number of factors delimiting its use and promotion. We find that
minor languages as mothertongue get in the way of achieving social status.
It is because of this that illiterate parents in India prefer to have their children
educated in a major language of the region rather than in the nonprestigious
and nonstandard mothertongue. Secondly, there are many minority languages
which have yet to be provided with even a practical orthography.

Providing a script to nonliterate languages has posed serious challenges to
language planners. It is interesting to note that, apart from many minor orthographic systems, there are ten major script systems commonly used in India.
In spite of the fact that Christian missionaries promoted the cause of Roman
script, the general trend has been that linguistic minorities opted for the
script system employed by the dominant language speakers of their region.
Thus, those linguistic minorities which are scattered in different linguistic
belts of India employ different script system despite their ethnic language
being one and the same. For example, the Santali language is written in four
distinct script systems – Devanagari, Bengali, Oriya, and Roman. Similarly,
Konkani which is written in Devanagari, Kannada, Malayalam, and Roman.

With ethnic minorities becoming more active in their resistance to majority
group domination, we find a distinct change in the trend. Linguistic minorities which are in search of their own "great tradition" find the use of the
script system, employed by the dominant superordinates at variance with
their drive for integration and consolidation. Consequently, we notice a
strong movement by the members of such speech groups to identify their
own indigenous script system with their ethnic identity. It is not surprising

therefore that supporters of the Santali movement are also promoters of the Santal script, better known as the Ol script.

The problem of selection of a script for nonliterate minority languages with "little tradition," however, is not yet resolved. There seem to be three competing choices — Devanagari (which is employed by the speakers of primary official languages of the Union), Roman (which is employed in the use of the associate official language), and the other eight major scripts (which are employed by the users of major nationality languages in their respective regions). There are also scholars who on the consideration of cross-linguistic communicability, cost measure in the technology of printing, and drive for national integrity, argue in favour of one script for all languages of India. The group which is against the idea of reducing all scripts to one believes that script systems in India, like their language counterparts, should be planned on the principle of "unity in diversity".

It is suggested that nonliterate languages should opt for the script employed by the major nationality languages of the region. This will smooth the way for those acquiring literacy in the mothertongue to switch over to literacy in the second language. This will also help the users of nonliterate languages to enter the mainstream of national life en route to the mainstream of regional life. In other words, this would integrate them both in the regional as well as the national life, which would not be the case if they were literate in the second language only. At the same time, it would decrease the load of learning another script, be it Devanagari or Roman, for their mothertongues.

In the pan-Indian perspective, this proposal with regard to the use of the script of the regional language for the mothertongue means promotion of multiscript for all Indian languages. The promotion of a multiscript system should neither be looked down upon as a burden on society nor as detrimental to its cultural or political progress. In fact, like multilingualism, script pluralism can prevent the depersonalization of society which would result in the case of only one script being used for all Indian languages.

Notes

1 The expression "linguistically organized" states means that now each state is identified with one dominant speech community. For example, Andhra Pradesh as a state is identified with the Telugu speech community. This community claims 85.37 % of the total population of the state on the Quantum dimension and on the power dimension enjoys administrative privileges because Telugu functions as the official language of the state.

By "speech community" we mean a group of people who show the following three characteristics: (1) members of the group are linked by some defined functioning of social organization; (2) they are able to communicate with each other, and (3) they share at least one language or linguistic variety as well as the norms for its use.

2   As the 1971 Census figures reveal, (divided) Maharashtra, Gujarat, (divided) Punjab, and Haryana States now have Marathi (76.61), Gujarati (89.39), Punjabi (79.49) and Hindi (89.42) speech communities, respectively, in dominant position. (The figures represent the percentage of speakers in their respective States.)

References

Apte, M. L. 1970. Some sociolinguistic aspects of interlingual communication in India. *Antropological Linguistics* XII. 3. 63–82.

Anderson, A. B. 1981. The problem of minority languages: reflections on the Glasgow Conference, *Language Problems & Language Planning* 5.3. 291-304.

Das Gupta, J. 1970. *Language conflict and national development.* Berkley: University of California Press.

Fishman, J. A. 1969. National language and languages of wider communication in developing nations, *Anthropological Linguistics* XI. 111-135.

Haugen, E. 1978. Bilingualism, language contact and immigrant languages in the United States: a research report. In: *Advances in the Study of Societal Multilingualism*, ed. by J. A. Fishman. 1-111. The Hague: Mouton.

Hymes, D. H. 1972. Foreword. In: M. Swadesh, *The origin and diversification of language.* London: Routledge and Kegan Paul.

Iyengar, K.R.S. 1973. The language problem of India. In: G. S. Reddi, ed. *The Language Problem of India.* Delhi: National Publishing House.

Lewis, E. G. 1972. *Multilingualism in the Soviet Union.* The Hague: Mouton.

Neustupný, J. V. 1974. The modernization of the Japanese system of communication, *Language in Society* 3.1. 35-50.

Misra, B. G. 1979. Language movements in the Hindi region, In: *Language Movements in India,* E. Annamalia, ed. Mysore: CIIL.

Pattanayak, D. P. 1981. *Multilingualism and mother-tongue education.* Delhi: Oxford University Press.

Pietersen, L. 1978. Issues and trends in Frisian bilingualism. In: J. A. Fishman, ed. *Advances in the Study of Societal Multilingualism,* The Hague: Mouton.

Srivastava, R. N. 1980. Societal bilingualism and problems in organizing language teaching in India, *Indian Journal of Applied Linguistics.* VI. 2. 13-37.

––– 1981. *The communicative roles of 'out-group' languages of India.* Paper submitted to the Second International Conference on 'Language and Local Government', held at Baku/USSR May 18-21, 1981.

––– 1982. *On the cross-conceptual diversity of linguistic terms.* Paper submitted to the International Conference on "In Search of Terminology", held at Mysore, January 1981.

Literacy and minorities: Divergent perceptions

J. V. NEUSTUPNÝ, *MONASH UNIVERSITY*

Contemporary social science has placed emphasis on variation both in social realities and in their perception by members of the society. The same emphasis is necessary in our approaches to literacy and minorities. The character of literacy and the ways we perceive it differ fundamentally in dependence on particular socioeconomic settings. So does the character of ethnic minorities.

Unless sociologists, sociolinguists and educators are prepared to fully accept this fact, it will be difficult not only to understand the relevant problems in societies other than our own, but also to communicate about literacy and minority issues across cultural boundaries. The questions of literacy and minorities are necessarily considered in different ways in a developing country of the Third World, such as Indonesia, and in a developed industrial nation of the type of the USA. Rapprochement is possible, but not before we acknowledge and interpret the existing differences.

A developmental typology working with socioeconomic types such as Traditional, Early Modern, Modern, and Contemporary will be basic to this paper (cf. Neustupný 1978, p. 27, 147-182, 255). I shall argue that the way societies at large and their representatives view literacy and minorities closely relates to the characteristics of their socioeconomic types. It should be understood that the typology I have in mind is a mere explanatory device and does not imply evaluations: a Contemporary society is not necessarily "better" than a Traditional one. Nor is a Traditional view of literacy or minorities necessarily "worse" than the assumptions and attitudes of people educated in a Contemporary Western environment.

*I would like to thank Michael Clyne and John Platt for a number of penetrating comments on this paper.

Literacy

1. Traditional Literacy

The designation "traditional society" is a rather rough tool with which to approach the large variety of social structures preceding the phenomenon of modernization. Among literate traditional societies, some limit the use of writing to ritual purposes and to basic practical tasks. In other societies, such as those of Ancient Greece, Medieval India, or China, written language further develops and appears widely as the vehicle of philosophy, literature, historiography, and the beginnings of science (Goody 1968). In the former type only a very small number of people possess literacy. In the latter the persons involved include a large number of specialists – for an average speaker, however, the skill of literacy is of no consequence. With Srivastava (cf. his contributions in this volume) we can speak of "nonliteracy" rather than "illiteracy".

The perception of the problem of literacy in traditional societies follows the pattern of the problem itself. Illiteracy is only noticed where literacy was expected. It is "natural" if someone who does not specialize in thought or administration, is unable to read and write. Khubchandani has aptly characterized this situation in noting that in traditional societies "literacy, no doubt, forms an important asset and accomplishment of an individual, but *not a necessary* condition of his survival and dignity (1981: 73-74). In Traditional societies nonliteracy is not treated as a major communication problem.

Although as a rule this way of perception changes in the Early Modern period, I wonder whether it disappears in full or perhaps survives in some strata of the society across the boundaries of socioeconomic change. Experience with gypsies in Czechoslovakia in the 1950s seems to support the possibility of survival. Illiteracy was viewed by them not as a fatal disease (as in other groups of the society) but as a natural state of affairs which did not warrant a special explanation or concern.

It may be appropriate to note here that while speaking of "perceptions" one must distinguish at least two different levels. Firstly, each potential communication problem can be perceived at the unconscious level: users of language may perceive their ignorance of spelling rules, experience uneasiness or frustration with regard to spelling problems, or even avoid certain words in order not to have to spell them. However, this does not imply that they would have to be aware of their problem.

The second type of "perception" is a conscious process, accompanied by articulated attitudes, theories, discussions, or policies. It is useful to realize that this type does not fully derive from the unconscious attitudes. Discussions of literacy or minorities are frequently influenced by established idioms and problem formulations, or by theoretical constructs originating in other cultures. For instance, most academics and top administrators in the present-day developing nations have studied or lived in the West. Although their unconscious perception of problems of their countries may remain unchanged, they are likely to employ legitimations and idioms which belong to a Western system. This fact may complicate the access of others to an exact picture of the relevant situation.

2. Early Modern literacy

With the beginning of industrialization traditional societies evolve into what I call Early Modern society. This socioeconomic type is characterized by a large number of social problems connected with the formation of modern nations, new social classes, and new social relationships between individuals.

Illiteracy now becomes a major problem. One reason why mastery of the written language matters is, as is often suggested, the need for literate manpower in industry and commerce. However, additional factors must be identified. It seems, for instance, that the process of individualization, which promotes each speaker to his own ideology-builder and manager, calls for radically increased competence in the written language and contributes in this way to the spread of literacy (cf. Slaughter 1982).

Final conclusions can only be drawn after a systematic analysis of the functions of the written language is available for all types of social structures. These functions are not universal, as anthropologists sometimes tacitly assume, but change with the socioeconomic type. For instance the extensive use of written language for making promises (commissive function), for establishing new situations (performative function), for instruction (instructional function) and for some other uses, sharply rise in the Early Modern period. On the other hand, keeping diaries and taking notes (self-regulative function) or writing letters to simply maintain contact (contact function) seem to weaken after the Early Modern period, at least in some societies (cf. Neustupný 1977).

In multiethnic states, it is principally in this period that the problem of literacy combines with the need to attain reading/writing competence in a linguistic variety different from the speaker's native variety. The issue, introduced in this volume by Coulmas, is connected with the problem of minorities which I shall discuss below.

The problem of literacy is, of course, actively perceived at this stage. General compulsory education is the universal policy designed as the corrective device. At the personal level of perception, illiteracy means lack of education and is evaluated negatively. Literacy is still far from being general or even universal. A large number of categories of language users who have not had access to good education remain illiterate. The term "restricted literacy" could be applied here, even if in a somewhat different sense from Goody's usage.

According to statistics quoted by Cipolla (1969: 127), in 1900, 23 % of the population of the Austrian Empire, 19 % of the population of Belgium, and 17 % in France could neither read nor write. Since these figures rely on self-assessment and exclude many of those who could do little else than sign their own name, the actual figures for functional illiteracy can be assumed to be much higher. In the USA, for the same period, the average rate of illiteracy has been reported as 10.7 %, but a considerable gap existed between the white and nonwhite population (6.2 % as opposed 44.5 %, cf. Wick 1980, p. 109).

Two excellent surveys of literacy conducted in Japan in 1948 and 1955-56 are of particular interest. At the time of these surveys Japan reached, in my interpretation, the very end of the Early Modern period. The results of the surveys well illustrate the phenomenon of "restricted literacy." Between 20 % and 50 % of Japanese language users were described as experiencing intense or noticeable problems in the use of the written language (cf. Monbusho 1961, Nomoto 1977).

TABLE 1: Rate of Illiteracy in Japan, 1955-56

	Tokyo area (rural)	North-Eastern Japan (rural)
No competence in reading characters	0.1	0.8
No reading/writing competence	9.5	15.7
Problems (sometimes serious) in the use of written language	48.3	61.5

Source: Monbusho 1961

Table 1 shows the percentage of people who experienced literacy problems in the 1955-56 survey. The survey covered subjects aged 14 to 26 in
two selected areas, Tokyo and Northern Japan. The percentage of total illiterates in the survey was less than 1 % in each of the two areas. On the other
hand those who were considered to "possess no competence in the use of the
written language" and were expected to experience serious problems, made up
approximately 10 % of the Tokyo sample and 15 % of the North-East Japan
sample. However, another 50% or 60%, respectively, were also judged to lack
sufficient competence, and some of these subjects definitely could be classified as functional illiterates.

If my interpretation of these data is correct, they mean among other
things that the countries of the Third World which are in the Early Modern
stage at present should not place much hope in general literacy. At the level
of perception, total literacy may be the goal. However, we should realize that
a high degree of industrialization can be reached on the level of "restricted
literacy". This is not to say that restricted literacy was beneficial to 19th
century Europe or to 20th century Japan, or that it would be the preferable
pattern in present-day Asia or Africa. But it may be a historical necessity.

3. Modern literacy

The process of modernization was finalized in most Western industrial nations
at the beginning of the 20th century. The basic structure of the industrial
society was now completed and the feeling that fundamental conflict issues
were solved pervaded the leading strata of the society. As shown in World
War I, the economic crisis of the late 1920s, the history of European fascism
and World War II, this was a daring assumption. Yet, at the level of perception and ideology, a conflict-less mood prevailed.

In this period the character of literacy undoubtedly changed. Since the
whole of the community, including rural areas, became incorporated into
industrial society, no easily predictable sectors marked by limited or zero
literacy remained. Instead, disadvantaged individuals or groups were affected
– immigrants, the blacks, the gypsies, school dropouts. Of course, differential
competence in the use of written language depending on social class remained
an undisputable fact. On the other hand, complete illiteracy, represented by
the inability to sign one's name, seems to have been radically reduced. On the
basis of our present experience we can guess that in Western developed
nations functional illiteracy existed throughout the Modern period at the
level of not less than 10-20 % of the adult population. In today's Japan, some
of the speakers who were counted as encountering problems in the 1955-56

survey continued their education and can be expected to have attained literacy (Nomoto 1977). Others may have improved through active participation in roles which require the use of written language. Yet a considerable number must still possess a very limited functional competence in reading and particularly in writing. The figure cannot be lower than 20 %.

However, as far as perception is concerned, the Modern period creates the myth of 99 % literacy for the industrialized societies of the world. Illiteracy is considered to be a very rare illness. The stigma of illiteracy is enormous. "Illiterate" now becomes synonymous not only with "uneducated" but also with "Ignorant" or "backward". Yet the fiction of the conflict-free society makes it unusual to raise the problem as an academic or political issue. Goody (1968: 1) reports on his colleagues of this period as follows:

> It is especially surprising that so little interest in literacy — and the means of communication in general — has been shown by social scientists. Those working in "advanced" societies have taken the existence of writing for granted . . . .

Let me note in addition that Cipolla's useful Pelican on illiteracy, published in 1969, reflects not only the changing mood by raising the issue, but also reflects the older (Modern) pattern by presenting literacy as a problem of the past, not of the present.

For an average Japanese intellectual any suggestion of widespread illiteracy appears dubious even today. He would be prepared to deduct a few per cent of the official 99 % figure, but not as much as appears to be necessary. Only those who have had the experience of working among the disadvantaged can break through the general mode of perception. However, the representative section of society, including the Education Ministry and the teachers unions, take general literacy for granted and show no interest in the problem. No new survey of literacy has been conducted since 1956.

4. Contemporary literacy

The perception of human society began changing again in the developed industrial nations as they were moving from the Modern to the Contemporary type of social structure. I believe that this process commenced in the 1960s and that it remains characteristic of the present period. After being denied existence throughout the Modern period, latent social problems reappear on the scene: problems of ethnic minorities, social class, poverty, sexual, and other discrimination, the problem of the human environment, and many others. Literacy is joining these issues, even if not in a spectacular way.

Firstly, the myth of the 99 % literacy seems to be gone, at least among experts. Specialized reliable surveys are still rare. However, in the case of the USA, Northcutt (1975) could conclude that in 1975 20 % of adult Americans were then "functionally incompetent" (could not perform basic operations such as reading/writing or simple calculations (see Copperman 1980). This figure included 8 % of higher income earners (over $18,000) and 40 % of those with incomes under $4,000. Copperman argues that in the mid-1960s, reading ability of American children actually began declining, compared with improvements in the immediately preceding period (Copperman 1980: 115). Our feeling is that the figures given by Copperman indicate a trend. If that is so, no single popular argument such as the spread of TV can account for the change of course. In order to understand this process, it will be necessary to survey the varying practical role of written language in work situations, as well as to consider the obvious change in the symbolic function of literacy: to be able to use the written language is no longer a symbol of belonging to a particular social class, while to be illiterate becomes more a practical problem than grounds for social stigma.

Still, the objective of universal literacy is retained. The current paradigm does not simply accept that a certain percentage of the population could remain without a sufficient command of the written language. This continues to be regarded as an undesirable situation that must be corrected.

Another novel feature of the contemporary approach is to look at literacy in terms of "functional literacy", "reading competence", or competence in the written language (cf. Coulmas' paper in this volume, also Slaughter 1982), rather than as the acquisition of a script, notably the alphabet. Concern with competence for interaction, rather than with the acquisition of inventories, is of course a general feature of Contemporary attitudes towards social facts.

In connection with a new attitude towards linguistic variation, emphasis is now shifting from acquiring literacy in the national language to acquiring literacy through the medium of one's native variety of language. This trend is conspicuous in the perception of literacy in the most highly developed countries. However, perception clearly precedes reality here, at least in the case of Australia. No more than a few lines are needed to enumerate Australian schools which have adopted this approach (Clyne 1982: 129).

For my argument, it is important to realize that the contemporary perception of literacy cannot be easily applied to the countries of the Third World which belong to the Early Modern type. It would be foolish to expect that these countries would finance programmes aimed at achieving 100 % literacy prior to establishing a socioeconomic structure that would require such objectives. The problem of "functional literacy" may be very different from the same problem in a developed country, and the immediate objectives may come close to the traditional aim of learning the script. Caution is also called for with regard to literacy programmes in minority languages. As Coulmas has already pointed out, such programmes may run, in Third World nations, against the need for national unity, and each case must be carefully considered on its own merits.

To carry out a literacy project in a developing country in accordance with the Contemporary perception of the problem might agree with our general sociopolitical persuasion. Still, I wonder whether even an ideal socialist society, in which all elites had been abolished and which was totally committed to equality and social justice, could succeed in this task.

For one thing, let us realize that the contemporary society is by no means an ideal structure in which all problems would be solved in accordance with the perceptions of its most advanced strata.

Minorities

1. Traditional variation

The term *minority* will be employed to refer to all ethnic communities which speak a variety of language other than a variety of the "national language" of the country. The usage is etymologically incorrect because a "minority" defined in this way can actually be a "majority", but it has been too well established to be changed. Strictly speaking, a minority is a category which only develops in an Early Modern nation. The number of varieties and their functional distribution in traditional societies presented a much more complex picture. The language of religion and ideology was not necessarily also the written language of administration. The language of literature was frequently different from both of these varieties. The spoken language of administration might be still another variety. Khubchandani (1981: 19-20) gives examples of Indian rural communities in which at least eight very different groups of varieties are in daily use.

With regard to attitudes towards language and perception of linguistic variation in Traditional societies my understanding owes much to Khubchandani. Although we did know that ethnic groups of pre-Modern Europe often lived side by side in the same communities without much friction, Khubchandani's picture of a "grass-root linguistic pluralism" has most eloquently illustrated the situation which differs so much from the experience of most Western linguists. His linguistic portrait of India shows a situation in which a large number of varieties, used by different people, or by the same people for different purposes, happily coexist and where "switching of linguistic codes from native speech to Hindi/Urdu is similar to switching of styles (such as informal/ formal) in monolingual situations" (Khubchandani 1981: 18). In his view, there is a strong trend in India to retain this pluralism and to reject attempts by the élites to elevate some of the varieties into the position of power — an act which automatically means that other varieties are relegated to the position of minority languages.

However, two questions of principle bear upon Khubchandani's picture of the Indian situation. Firstly, we must ask to what extent his pluralism is still typical for the India of today. Khubchandani's own discussions seem to indicate that this traditional arrangement has been significantly weakened and is being replaced by a hierarchical system, for which a negative evaluation of variation is characteristic.

Second, Khubchandani attempts to relate the Indian situation to some contemporary perceptions of Western societies. Undoubtedly, similarities such as the positive evaluation of linguistic variation are apparent. However, it can be questioned whether the surface similarity should be interpreted in the same way. The entire historical context is different. I would be delighted if the developing nations of today could avoid the traumatic experience of the European modernization process, but I am less confident than Khubchandani that this can be done.

The traditional nonevaluative perception may, however, survive in individual cases in the Early Modern (developing) stage. I wonder whether this does not contribute to an occasional lack of interest among ethnic minorities in the question of the national language in which literacy is offered. In such cases the new national language is perhaps perceived as *just another* functional variety within the pluralistic system, not as *the dominant* variety of the forthcoming period. When the mistake is discovered, it may be too late to take counteraction.

2. Early Modern variation

The Early Modern period is the era of industrialization and the establishment of a sociopolitical structure which is to support the industrial economic base. As far as linguistic variation is concerned, some of the varieties of the pre-Modern systems are reduced. For instance the H-standards, which characterize what C. A. Ferguson has called *diglossia,* receive their final blow. On the other hand, one variety is now elevated to the position of the "national language", and within this language a considerable number of sub-varieties (the language of modern administration, law, science, technology, etc) develop. This new "national language" becomes the sole vehicle of the unification of the national networks and of social development. It also serves as the sole vehicle of education and literacy.

There are, of course, examples of developing societies with two or more "national languages", both in 19th century Europe and among the present-day developing nations. The Austrian Empire, prior to 1918, and contemporary Singapore, with English, Chinese, Malay, and Tamil as its "national languages", belong to this category. However, even in these societies the hierarchical arrangement among the "national languages" exists, *de facto* if not *de jure* (see Platt and Weber 1980: 39 on the position of English and other languages of education in Singapore); a large number of other varieties which have not made it to the "national language" are simply excluded.

In the case of Early Modern Japan (mid-19th century till after WWII) the assimilation policies of the mainstream of society were in no way less drastic than those we know from Early Modern Europe. Minorities such as the Ainu or, after 1911, the Koreans were emphatically suppressed, with the Ainu being almost totally assimilated and the Koreans, too strong for assimilation, reestablishing their national independence after 1945.

It is fair to admit that national unity in this period is a fragile flower which needs gentle care. It is equally necessary to realize that the leaders of the more powerful ethnic groups do attempt to secure as strong a territorial and population basis as possible; and while pursuing their policies, do not stop at any form of oppression.

The public perception of variation is twofold. Representatives of the national establishment evaluate negatively any competing variety; members of minority groups, to the extent that they are capable of resistance, fight back. What happened in Europe towards the end of the 19th century and at the beginning of the present century is now happening in the Third World. History repeats itself, not exactly, but to a recognizable degree. There are special cases and new features due to differences in the international environment. However, the overall trend is necessarily the same.

3. Modern variation

In a Modern Society the mainstream ethnic group has established itself, at the level of economic and political interaction, beyond any doubt. Some of the deviant minority groups have been almost totally destroyed, at least as linguistic entities (the Ainu in Japan), some fatally weakened and silenced (the Sorbs in Germany), others have formed separate national states. Variation and conflict still exist, even if to the mainstream group it appears to be of little significance. The ideology of nationalism is not needed any more and recedes to the background. The Western world of the first half of this century up to the 1960s and contemporary Japan (since the 1960s) are typical examples of Modern nations.

The Modern period sees the zenith of the flourishing of the "national languages" which are actively "cultivated" but not radically reformed. Emphasis is not on change (as in the preceding period), but on mere elaboration and maintenance of the status quo.

In 1980 Japan had well over half a million Koreans, over 50 thousand people of Chinese parentage, and it is estimated that approximately 30 thousand people considered themselves Ainu. Yet, the myth of the total ethnic homogeneity of the country maintained an absolute dominance in the public image. Discrimination against the Koreans has not been based on any explicitly formulated ideologies, but has remained widespread. There has been no official support for activities of any of the mentioned groups, nor for any facilities for education in their ethnic language.

This situation reminds us, among other things, of the case of Australia in the 1950s and 1960s. Although no reliable data are available for this period regarding the size of minority communities, on the basis of later figures (Clyne 1976) it can be inferred that approximately one-third of Australia's population were immigrants or children of immigrants, or Australian Aborigines, close to half of them from non-English-speaking backgrounds. Still, the official story, believed by almost everyone, was that of a basically homogeneous country, in which no minority problems existed.

Although there were few active discrimination policies (apart from cases such as excluding citizens with non-English backgrounds from recruitment into the Australian diplomatic service), the immigrant minorities were *de facto* the subject of discrimination in many forms (cf. Clyne 1982, p. 117). The attitude of the mainstream public was inimical to "foreign" languages. Speaking a language other than English in a public place could evoke angry comments. Immigrant children tried to hide at school the fact that they spoke a "foreign" language at home. Some limited facilities for learning English were available, but the teaching of the languages of immigrants was almost nonexistent.

In other words, at the level of discussions, theories, and organized policies, the Modern period shows a passive attitude to language variation. The hierarchical order in the society has already been established and needs no reinforcement of this kind. On the other hand, in actual social interaction, variation receives strong negative marking. It is interesting to note that this marking is mutual and universal: immigrants are held in contempt by the mainstream population, while they themselves despise the mainstream groups as well as other immigrants.

4. *Contemporary variation*

The situation started changing in the USA and other countries of the developed world in the 1960s. This is when the power of various sidestream groups in the society grew to such an extent that they could not be overlooked any more. The pendulum swung. To be different became the "in" thing. The picture that society held of itself could not but follow these new developments.

One warning is appropriate here. When social scientists spoke of modernization in the 1950s and early 1960s they often assumed that "modern" stood for "correct" or "perfect". For them the world was moving towards the aim of a "modern" society, beyond which no further improvements could be envisaged. Today we can look at modernization and Modern societies through more critical eyes, with an emphasis on their limitations and failures. The mistaken self-perception should not be repeated in the case of the Contemporary society. It must not be looked upon as an example of a perfect rational structure in which all problems have been solved and which represents the ultimate word in the organization of human society.

In the Australia of the 1970s, ethnic minorities were rediscovered. The fact that Australia is a multicultural and multilingual society is today a fact beyond any doubt for anyone. Yet the relationship between the mainstream and the sidestreams is not one of equality. The policy of assimilation has formally been abandoned, but in practice may of the assimilation processes continue to be in force. Budgets have been made available for the teaching of English to newcomers and for the teaching of ethnic languages. A large number of minority languages have been accepted as examination subjects for entry into universities. The symbolic value of these measures is considerable, but the teaching itself remains underdeveloped. Children who speak an ethnic language have come to be proud of being multilingual, even if there are differences between those whose ethnic language is Japanese (a high prestige language in present-day Australia) and those who speak an Italian dialect at home. Attitudes of the mainstream part of the community in daily interaction have improved to a considerable extent, but the fear of a possible future backlash exists.

The USA was admittedly first in developing the Contemporary system. The changes in Europe seem to be much slower, and the system is still very weak in Japan. Since its growth is dependent upon the absence of the danger of separatism and the availability of a part of the national income for redistribution to the minority groups, I do not expect that similar developments could be wholeheartedly pursued by those governments of the Third World which are not in a position to take the risk and to accept the expenditures.

Social scientists of the Contemporary world are proud of their new perception which acknowledges the existence of variation and social conflict, and do not hesitate to recommend it to the attention of their colleagues in the Third World countries. As long as this marks the beginning of a discussion, no objection can be raised. However, care must be taken in the case of attempts which aim simply at a transplantation of the Contemporary perception. This is where doubts concerning the Contemporary system are felt most strongly.

Are we absolutely sure that the retention of all minority languages will better the world? Why should this be so? Are we sure that children are not disadvantaged when they have to start their education in one language and shift later into another one? Are we doing enough to ensure that multilingualism within our own communities is based on a consistent multicultural policy? Which of the negative features of the Modern paradigm have not yet been affected? Is this resistance the result of change factors or does it originate in some inadequacies of our own paradigm?

As in the case of literacy, there should be no question of promulgating our current perceptions as the universal truth. A dialogue is necessary. Its result should be not merely to institute policies in nations of the Third World, but also to make sure that the Western societies are doing their best under the most favourable conditions in which they themselves operate.

References

Cipolla, C. M. 1969 *Literacy and Development in the West.* Harmondsworth: Penguin Books.

Clyne, M. G. 1976 *"Immigrant Languages" in Australia.* Hobart: University of Tasmania. (Public Policy Paper 6.)

――― 1982 *Multilingual Australia. Resources – Needs – Policies.* Melbourne: River Seine Publications.

Copperman, D. 1980 The decline of Literacy. *Journal of Communication* 30/1, 113-122.

Goody, J. (ed.) 1968 *Literacy in Traditional* Societies. Cambridge: Cambridge University Press.

Khubchandani, L. M. 1981 *Language, Education, Social Justice.* Poona: Centre for Communication Studies.

Monbusho, 1961 *Kokumin no yomikaki nooryoku.* Tokyo: Monbusho.

Neustupný, J. V. 1977 Nihongo no naka no kakikotoba no ichi [The position of the written language in Japanese]. *Gendai sakubun kooza* 1, 213-250. Tokyo: Meiji shoin.

――― 1978 *Post-Structural Approaches to Language.* Tokyo: University of Tokyo Press.

Nomoto, K. 1977 Nihonjin no yomikaki nooryoku. [Japanese reading/writing competence]. *Iwanami kooza Nihongo* 3, 39-69. Tokyo: Iwanami shoten.

Northcutt, N. 1975 *Adult Functional Competency: A Summary.* Austin: The University of Texas.

Platt, John, and Heidi Weber 1980 *English in Singapore and Malaysia*. Kuala Lumpur: Oxford University Press.
Slaughter, M. M. 1982 Literacy and development. MS.
Wick, T. 1980 The pursuit of universal literacy. *Journal of Communication* 30/1, 107-112. 107-112.

Index

Index of Subjects